FLY
TYING
FOR BEGINNERS

PETER GATHERCOLE

FLY
TYING
FOR BEGINNERS

HOW TO TIE 50 FAILSAFE FLIES

BARRON'S

A Quarto Book

First edition for North America published in 2006 by Barron's
Educational Series, Inc.

All inquiries should be addressed to:
Barron's Educational Series, Inc.
250 Wireless Boulevard
Hauppauge, NY 11788
www.barronseduc.com

ISBN-13: 978-0-7641-5845-2
ISBN-10: 0-7641-5845-7
Library of Congress Catalog Card Number 2005921781

QUAR.FTB

Conceived, designed, and produced by
Quarto Publishing plc
The Old Brewery
6 Blundell Street
London N7 9BH

Project Editor Paula McMahon
Art Editor Stephen Minns
Designer Anthony Cohen, Michelle Stamp
Assistant Art Director Penny Cobb
Copy Editor Carol Baker
Photographer Peter Gathercole
Proofreader Robert Harries
Indexer Pamela Ellis

Art Director Moira Clinch
Publisher Paul Carslake

Manufactured by Modern Age, Hong Kong

Printed by Midas Printing International Limited, China

9 8 7 6 5 4 3 2

Contents

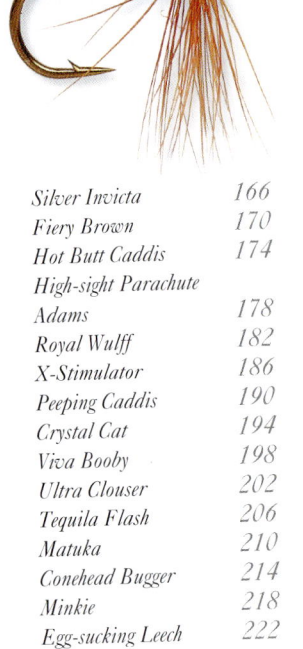

Introduction

Tying your first fly can seem like a daunting process at first. Along with the need to master new skills, questions such as which materials to use or hook to choose make it seem more complicated than it really is. By using step-by-step photographs and easy to understand captions, Fly Tying for Beginners answers the questions that plague both novices and more experienced fly tiers.

The book is designed to give the reader a comprehensive grounding in the key processes of fly tying. It starts with a thorough description of core techniques—building blocks you can use when tying many of the most effective artificial flies.

How to use this book

By introducing 15 core techniques, followed by 50 of the top artificial flies, and showing not only how they are tied but also the materials being used, the reader is guided smoothly through this process. All of the major fly groups are represented, including: nymphs and bugs, wet flies, dry flies, streamers, and hairwings.

Core Techniques

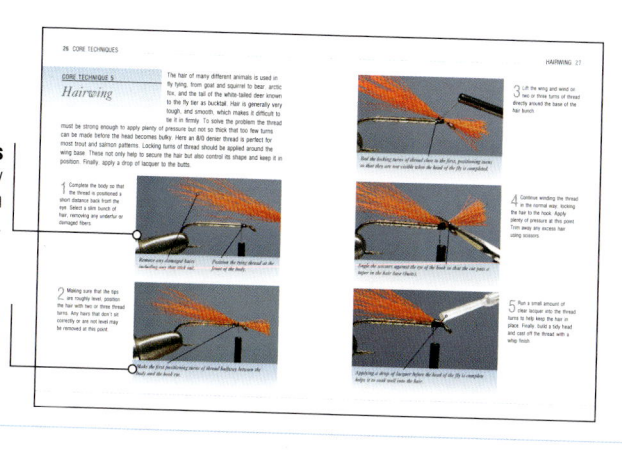

Step-by-step photographs
Each technique is clearly demonstrated in five steps, with sequential images and captions.

Annotation
Each step is annotated, referring to a specific part shown on the fly.

Fly Directory

How to use the fly
To understand how each fly is to be fished, there are icons showing whether it floats or sinks.

Recipe
Find details of the hook, thread, and other materials here.

Materials
The materials are shown in color, so the reader will have no doubt as to the type, form, and color being used, or where they are used on the fly.

Finished fly
A large full-color photograph of the finished fly shows a high level of detail.

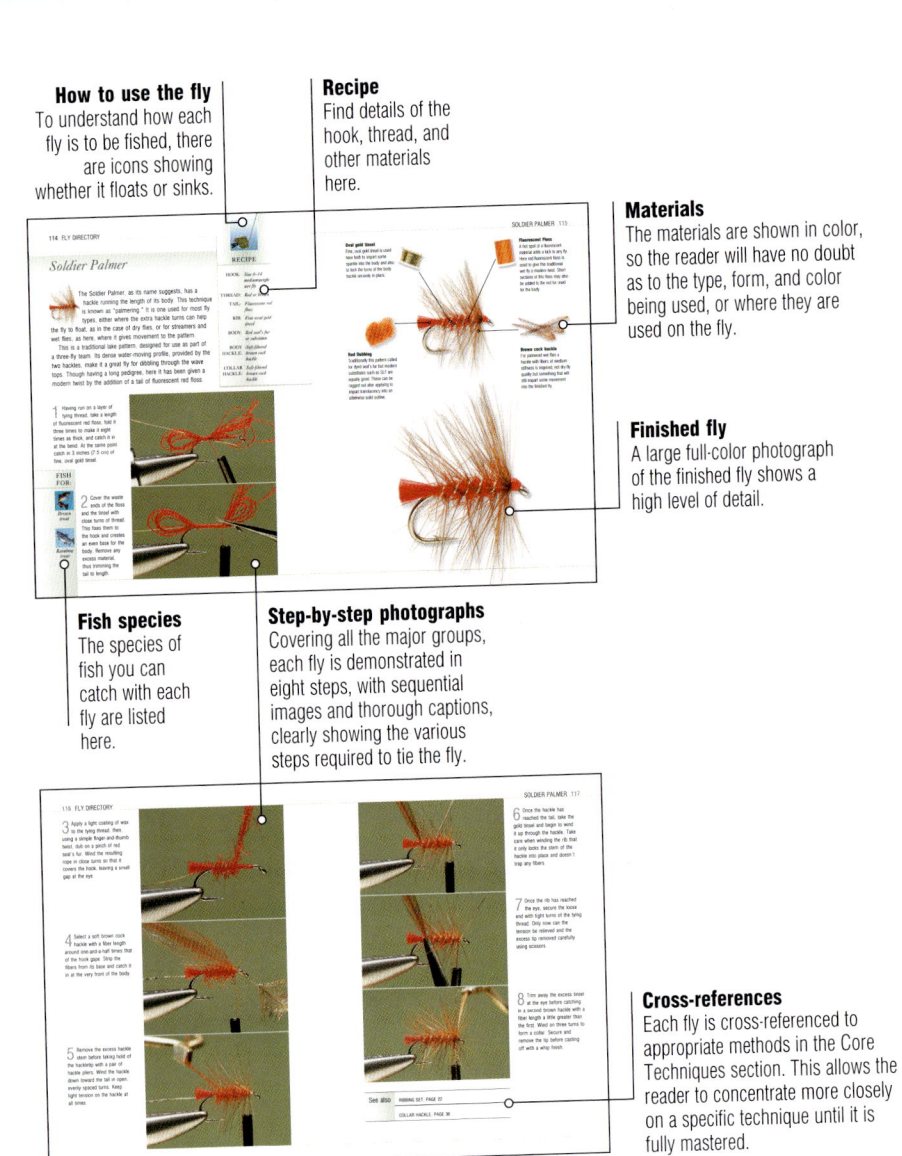

Fish species
The species of fish you can catch with each fly are listed here.

Step-by-step photographs
Covering all the major groups, each fly is demonstrated in eight steps, with sequential images and thorough captions, clearly showing the various steps required to tie the fly.

Cross-references
Each fly is cross-referenced to appropriate methods in the Core Techniques section. This allows the reader to concentrate more closely on a specific technique until it is fully mastered.

Tools

When selecting a set of fly-tying tools, there is no need to purchase every gizmo on the market. A far better idea is to concentrate on a few important items: those that will be used every time you sit at your tying bench.

It is possible to tie most flies using only a vise and a pair of scissors, but there are one or two extra items that will make the job much easier. Two must-haves are a **bobbin holder** and **hackle pliers**. A **dubbing twister** and a **hair-stacker** are good to have also.

One tip when choosing tools is never to go for the cheapest. A vise that won't hold a hook securely, or scissors with blades that don't meet, only lead to frustration. While as a beginner, purchasing top-of-the-range tools is an unnecessary expense, going for something more middle of the road that is well made and functional will pay off in the end.

VISE

The vise is the most important tool for any fly-tier because it lets you hold even a very small hook securely, so that the materials can be applied. There are various types of vise available, but a simple lever-action model with a table clamp, is the best one to start with, being both cheap and easy to use. The rotating collar allows the gap in the jaws to be adjusted to accommodate hooks of various sizes, while the lever ensures that adequate pressure can be applied to hold the hook firmly in place.

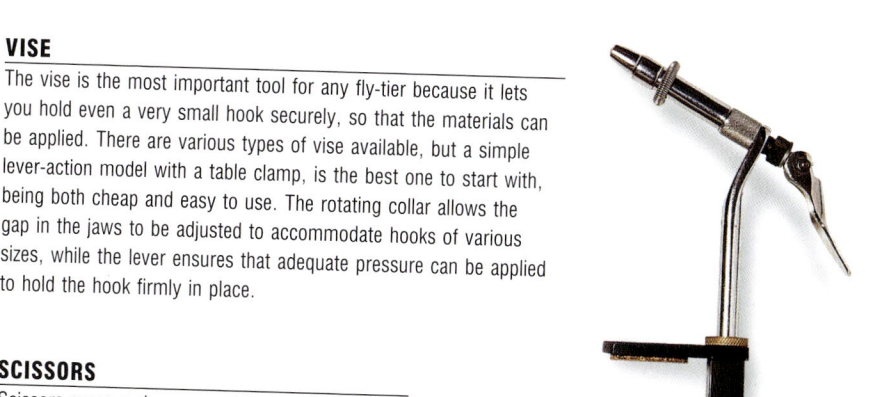

SCISSORS

Scissors come a close second in the rank of must-have fly-tying tools. They should have short, sharp points that meet properly, allowing precise cuts to be made. The only thing better than one pair of scissors is two pairs. Use one tough pair for cutting hair and tinsel; and a second, finer-bladed pair for the delicate trimming of hackles and threads.

HACKLE PLIERS

Hackle pliers are designed to hold a hackle securely in place while it is being wound. Choose a simple model with solid-sprung arms and jaws that are smooth; this will help prevent them from cutting the delicate hackle stems. Hackle pliers can also be used for winding chenille and other body materials.

HAIR STACKER

When creating wings from natural hair such as bucktail or squirrel tail, it can prove tricky to get all the tips of the fibers level. This simple little tool solves the problem: simply place the hair bunch, tips first, in the tube then tap lightly on a hard, flat surface and all the hairs should fall to the same level. Don't overdo the effect; the wing should still be slightly tapered and shouldn't look like a paintbrush.

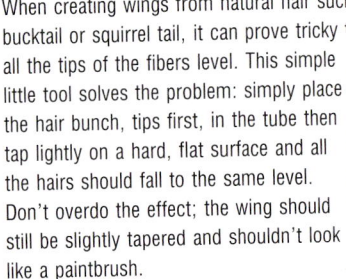

BOBBIN THREADER

Most times the bobbin holder can be threaded by simply pushing the end of the thread into the tube, then sucking. However, there are times when this is insufficient, for example, when thread is very thin or the bobbin holder's tube is clogged with wax. Here, a fine-wire loop on a short handle provides a foolproof alternative to doing things the old-fashioned way.

DUBBING NEEDLE

This simple tool has a number of uses, including teasing out dubbing materials, dividing wing slips, and freeing trapped hackle fibers. It is also used to apply lacquer to the head of a fly.

DUBBING TWISTER

This is an indispensable tool when creating dubbing loops. The two sprung arms hold the thread loop open so that the dubbing can be applied easily. A simple spin of the knurled wheel, and the tool twists the fur into a tight rope ready to be wound onto the hook.

BOBBIN HOLDER

This tool holds a bobbin of thread or floss, allowing it to be applied seamlessly to the hook and keeping waste to a minimum. The sprung metal arms retain just enough tension so that the thread feeds off easily when wound, but stays in place when the holder is released. Choose a spigot-type with a tube for precise application, and ensure that the tube is made from a smooth material, preferably ceramic, to prevent the thread from becoming frayed.

WHIP-FINISH TOOL

A perfectly good whip finish can be executed with fingers alone; however, some tiers find this specially designed tool a great help. Models vary, but most whip-finish tools have a straight handle with a hook at one end and, lower down, a sprung-wire arm. The tying thread is positioned over the tool's hook and arm and the resulting loop wound around the fly hook.

Materials

The hook forms the backbone of a fly, providing a rigid skeleton to which you will attach the materials, and more importantly, forms the link between the angler's line and the fish. The materials give the fly its form and influence how it will be fished. Depending on the types of materials used they can impart movement, imitate anything from a fish's body to the tiny legs of an insect, or determine whether the fly floats or sinks.

HOOKS

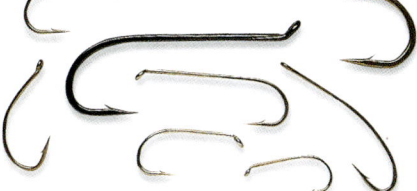

Hooks are available in a vast range of shapes and sizes to cater to the many and varied types of fly that can be created. The most popular are the standard round-bend hooks with either a turned-down or turned-up eye. These are used primarily for tying wet flies, nymphs, and dry flies.

Not only does the size of the hook gape (the distance between the hook point and its shank) vary, but so too does the shank length. Using long shanks allows even big flies to be tied on hooks with a relatively small gape.

Other specialist hooks such as Living Larva, Caddis, and Grub Hooks are shaped more like a nymph or pupa and help create a fly with a realistic profile.

The three main colors, or finishes, are bronze, silver, or black in the case of salmon or steelhead hooks.

HACKLES

Hackles are used for the vast majority of flies. In dry flies, they help keep the fly floating, while in wet flies and nymphs, they suggest the legs of an insect and provide movement. They are even used as wings in streamer patterns.

Most hackles come from domestic fowl, both the hen or cock bird. The neck and saddle are the areas where the correct type of feather grows. Those of the hen are softer and more webby, and are most effective for use on flies intended to sink. The cock bird has stiffer, less absorbent feathers and provides the highest quality dry-fly hackle. Selectively bred "genetic" hackles are the best, though they aren't cheap, with some saddle hackles long enough to tie up to ten flies.

DUBBING

Originally the body hair of animals such as rabbit, hare, muskrat, and baby seal provided the various textures of fur used to create dubbed bodies. Although these are still used today, there are numerous manmade alternatives available, some even with a trilobal construction to mimic the texture of real fur.

Dubbing is available in a wide range of colors and textures, and either in single colors and materials, or as blends. The latter are often a combination of natural and manmade products.

FEATHERS

Apart from hackles, a huge variety of other types of bird plumage is used in fly tying, from duck feathers to those of the turkey, goose, pheasant, partridge, and peacock to name a few. One of the most widely used feathers is marabou, a soft, mobile plume that comes from the domestic turkey.

HAIR AND FURS

Tough and resilient, the hair from animals such as the white-tailed deer, which gives us bucktail, plus elk, squirrel, rabbit, and mink, provides a ready supply of winging material. Hair may be used either in bunches, or, as with rabbit, used in strips still on the skin. The softer underfur of rabbit, hare, and muskrat may also be used as dubbing. Various species of deer also provide a hollow body hair that is used for tying Muddlers.

THREADS AND FLOSSES

Thread is used to fix the materials used to create a fly securely to the hook. Most threads are made from nylon and are available in a huge range of colors both plain and fluorescent. Thread also comes in a variety of diameters: 8/0 is the finest, and is used for the smallest dry flies and nymphs, while the thicker 6/0 is a general-purpose thread used for most types of fly. For big streamers and salmon flies, the thread of choice is 3/0, which is strong enough to hold tough materials, such as hair, firmly in place.

Depending on the brand, thread comes both plain and prewaxed.

Floss is much thicker than thread, but is available in similar colors. Rayon is the most popular type; being smooth and shiny makes it ideal for tying flat, lump-free bodies on a variety of dry flies, wet flies, and streamers.

TINSELS AND WIRES

Tinsels are available in two materials—metal and plastic. Metal is still widely used, especially for round and oval tinsels. These are used primarily on wet flies and streamers either as a rib or a complete body. However, the main drawback of metal tinsel is that it tarnishes, so plastics such as Mylar, that retain their shine indefinitely, are now used more widely.

Tinsels come in a wide range of colors and effects, both spooled and in hanks. The latter type is used widely to give a sparkling effect to wings and tails.

Originally available only in gold, silver, and copper, wires are now available in a range of colors and diameters, and may be used either as ribbing, or to form the bodies of quick-sinking nymphs.

PLASTICS

These manmade products are available in a wide range of forms, from microcellular foam to thin, flexible strips and strands. Their main attributes are that they are tough and often translucent, making them great both for ribbing or entire bodies on nymphs and streamers.

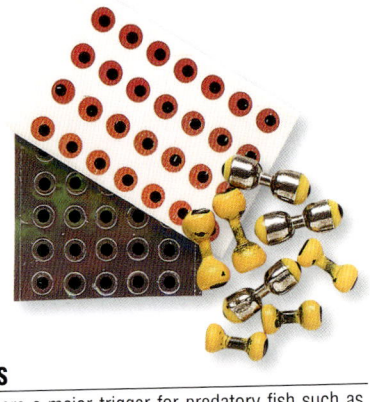

WOOL AND YARNS

Wool and yarns are used primarily to form the bodies on a range of wet-fly and streamer patterns. They include ordinary sheep's wool, manmade products such as Antron, and thick, chunky yarns such as chenille, which is great for tying both streamers and big, chunky nymphs. Much finer chenilles are also available, which can be used on hooks as small as a size 16.

EYES

Eyes are a major trigger for predatory fish such as trout. The easiest and cheapest eyes to use are stick-on decals, which are available in a range of sizes, colors, and finishes. They are lightweight and are perfect for patterns designed to fish near the surface. If you need to add weight, there is little to beat lead dumbbell eyes. These are available in a range of sizes and can be painted or left plain.

BEADS

Small beads are commonly used in a wide range of nymph patterns and for a few streamers. Metal beads are available in a range of colors, including gold, silver, copper, and black, plus some fluorescent colors, such as orange and chartreuse. They are usually fixed at the hook eye, providing weight—particularly the tungsten beads—and, in the case of the more colorful types, a bit of sparkle. The lighter glass and plastic beads are used either to create the eyes on imitations of large nymphs or to add extra flash to the fly.

WAX

Wax is used to coat the tying thread, making it sticky, which helps fur and other materials adhere to it. Plain beeswax may be used, but there are a variety of purpose-designed products available as well.

Core Techniques

In any practical craft, there is usually a set of techniques around which the whole practice is built. This book starts with three important basic techniques and moves onto the core techniques that crop up time and time again, forming the building blocks for the art of fly-tying.

BASIC TECHNIQUE 1

Securing the thread

The first crucial step is attaching the thread firmly to the hook. The strength of a fly is built on the solid foundation of thread, so it is important to get this technique right. This simple procedure, when practiced, will become second nature, and once you have been tying flies for a week or two, it will be undertaken with hardly a thought.

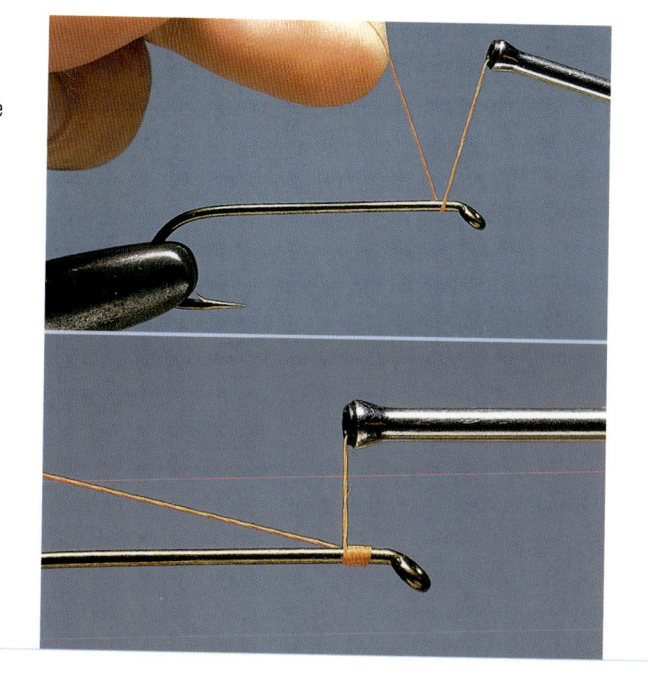

1 With the hook secured in the vise, loop the thread under the hook shank. Hold the loose end tight and bring both it and the end closest to the bobbin holder above the hook to form a V-shape.

2 Wind the thread closest to the bobbin holder, down the hook shank using the turns to trap the loose end held in the fingers. Make five or six turns until the end is secured, then remove the waste. Add further close turns to form a solid base.

BASIC TECHNIQUE 2

Lacquering the head

Though not absolutely necessary, a drop of lacquer applied to the completed head both protects the exposed thread turns and produces a smooth finish. This is especially the case in larger flies, where a smooth shiny head finishes the fly off beautifully.

1 Having completed the head, apply a coat of clear lacquer using the tip of a dubbing needle. Allow the lacquer to soak well into the thread turns.

2 Add two or three more coats until the head is smooth and shiny. After each coat, ensure that the eye is kept clear by running a length of nylon or a stripped hackle stem through it.

3 Allow the coats of lacquer to set before using the fly. If applying a coat of black lacquer, always use a coat of clear first to prevent the color from bleeding into the materials.

BASIC TECHNIQUE 3

Whip finish

It is important when tying a fly to begin with a solid foundation. And once that fly is complete, it is equally important that it should be finished off securely. There is nothing more frustrating than having a fly unravel, especially at the waterside, all for the want of a neatly executed whip finish.

While it is possible to get away with a few simple half-hitches and a drop of lacquer, by far the best way to ensure that your fly lasts as long as possible is by applying a three- or five-turn whip finish.

In essence, the whip finish is merely a series of thread turns made to form a running loop. This is applied close to the hook-eye and when drawn tight, locks the loose end of the thread securely in place. It can be accomplished either by using the fingers or a specially designed tool—and time spent practicing the procedure is never wasted.

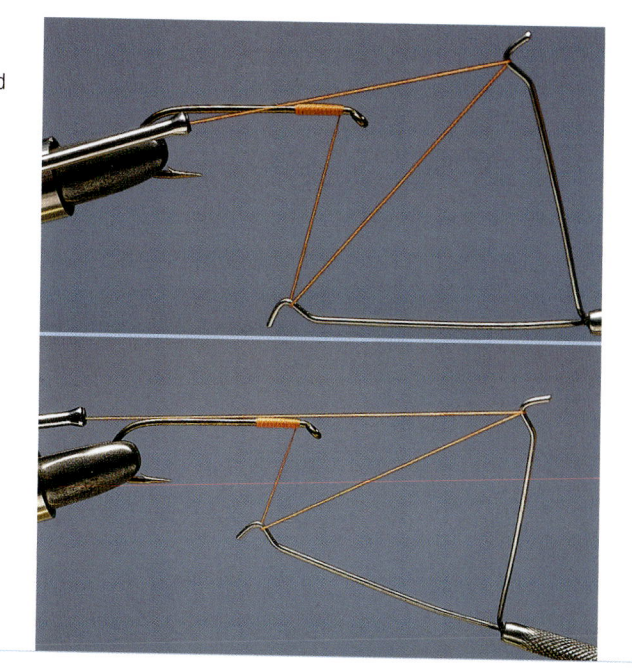

1 Assuming that the fly is complete, the thread should be positioned at the hook-eye. Next, loop the thread first over the straight arm, then over the one that projects at a right angle from the tool's stem.

2 Drop the tool slightly, so that the end of the tying thread coming from the bobbin holder is positioned in line with the hook shank. This forms a triangle shape with the thread.

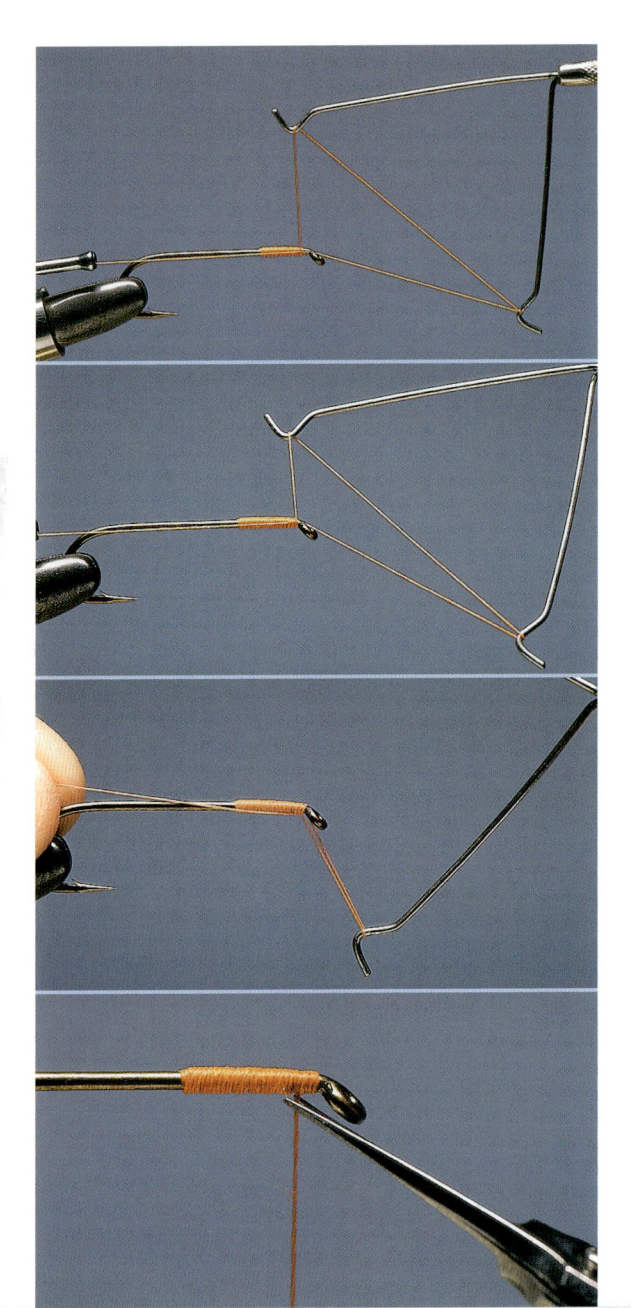

3 Now twist the tool half a turn so that the straight arm is positioned above the hook. This turn locks the loose end of the thread.

4 Repeat the procedures outlined in steps two and three. This produces a series of turns that secure the loose end of the tying thread. Between three and five turns are enough for most flies.

5 Once the turns have been applied, pull on the loose end of the thread coming from the bobbin holder. This will draw the loop closed. While doing this, flip off the thread from the straight arm, retaining tension with the angled arm alone.

6 When the loop is almost closed, remove the final arm of the whip-finish tool and pull the thread tight. Now simply trim away the loose end of the thread with scissors.

Parachute Hackle

This is a dry fly/emerger technique designed to create a fly that sits with its body below the surface supported by a hackle. Flies tied in the parachute style are used to imitate small mayflies or caddis flies hatching at the surface and prove deadly when fish are feeding on items just under the surface. To achieve the parachute profile, the hackle is wound around a post projecting from the top of the hook. This post can be fashioned from the hackle itself or more usually as a wing made from foam, CDC (cul-de-canard), or polypropylene. This not only helps the fly to float but also acts as a "sighter," allowing the angler to see the fly even when it is sitting so low in the water.

1 Form a base of thread one-third of the way back from the eye. Divide a strand of polypropylene yarn in half lengthways and catch it in at its midpoint. Draw the two ends of the yarn together and wind on close turns of thread.

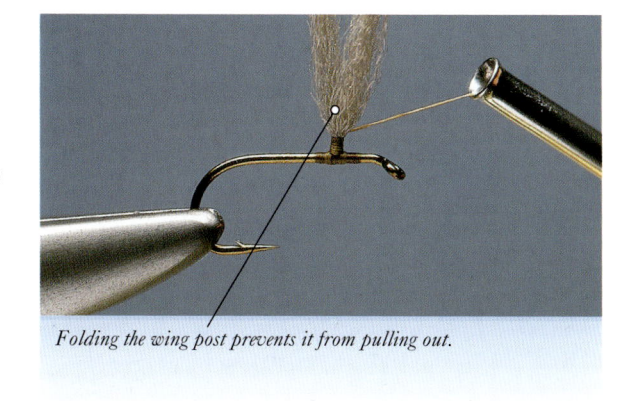

Folding the wing post prevents it from pulling out.

2 Carry the thread a short distance up the yarn to create a short, stiff section. Prepare the hackle by stripping the fibers from its base and catch it in at the base of the wing post.

Catch in the hackle so that the tip projects above the hook.

Add close turns of thread to form a stiff section onto which the hackle will be wound.

Secure the hackle stem with further thread turns.

Gently take hold of the hackletip with hackle pliers.

3 Take the hackle by its tip and begin winding it around the base of the wing post. Two or three turns is normally ample, though more may be applied if a denser effect is required.

Wind the hackle in close turns, working down the wing post.

Secure the hackletip with tying thread.

4 When the hackle has been wound, secure the loose tip with tying thread and remove the excess.

Remove the excess hackletip using scissors.

Cast off the thread with a whip finish made on the underside of the wound hackle.

5 Finally, trim the wing post to the desired length with scissors before casting off the thread with a whip finish wound beneath the turns of hackle.

CORE TECHNIQUE 2

Spinner Wing

One of the classic wing profiles for dry fly patterns is the spinner or "spent" wing. The aim here is to imitate the way the wings of an adult female mayfly, known to anglers as a spinner, spread out when trapped on the water's surface. This occurs when the insect has laid its eggs and then dies, hence the alternative term—spent. When large falls of these insects take place, trout become very specific in their feeding and will take only an imitation that is tied with outstretched rather than upright wings. Various materials can be used to imitate the spinner wing from hackletips to CDC and polypropylene.

1 Fix the hook in the vise and run on close turns of tying thread to form a solid base for the wing. Take a length of light gray or white polypropylene yarn.

On small patterns divide the polypropylene yarn lengthways to reduce bulk.

2 Offer the yarn up to the topside of the hook so that it lies along the hook shank. Fix in place with tight thread turns made halfway along the yarn.

Position the yarn approximately one-third of the hook's length back from the eye.

Make sure that the ends of yarn sit perfectly at 90 degrees to the hook shank.

Apply figure-of-eight turns of thread evenly around the base of the wings.

3 Twist the yarn so that it is now positioned at right angles to the hook shank. Apply figure-of-eight turns of thread around the wing base to fix it in position.

Always cut the wings together with a single snip of the scissors.

4 Once the wing is firmly secured, draw the two ends together above the shank and trim so that they are of equal length. The wings should each be slightly longer than the hook shank.

Spread the fibers of yarn to produce a thin, flat wing.

5 Wind the thread back up the shank toward the place where it was first caught in. Continue winding it right up to a point just short of the eye and secure the loose end.

Ribbing Set

Ribbing performs two main functions. It protects body materials and also locks the turns of a body hackle in place. It can also be used to add sparkle or to suggest the segmentation of an invertebrate's body. Various materials may be used for ribbing from traditional products such as metal tinsels or wires to nylon monofilament or plastic threads.Though lighter products such as nylon are more suitable when tying dry flies, many wet fly and streamer patterns still incorporate metal in the form of wire or round and oval tinsels that are constructed around a supporting core. Though the width and texture of these materials vary, the technique for applying them is basically the same.

1 Having fixed the hook in the vise, run the tying thread down to the bend and catch in any necessary tail material. Take 2-inch (5-cm) medium, oval gold tinsel.

Choose a tinsel width to complement the hook size. The tinsel should never dominate the body of the fly.

2 Catch in the tinsel at the base of the tail with two or three tight turns of thread. Allow the waste ends of the tinsel and the tail material to lie along the shank.

Catch in the tinsel at the same point that any tail material was caught in.

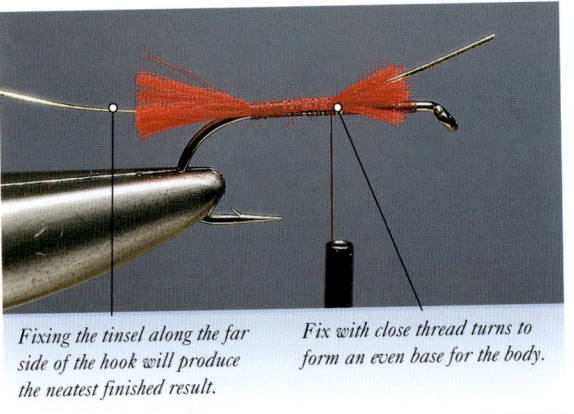

Fixing the tinsel along the far side of the hook will produce the neatest finished result.

Fix with close thread turns to form an even base for the body.

3 Using close turns of thread, secure the two materials along the hook shank. This procedure is very important as it forms an even base on which to apply any body material.

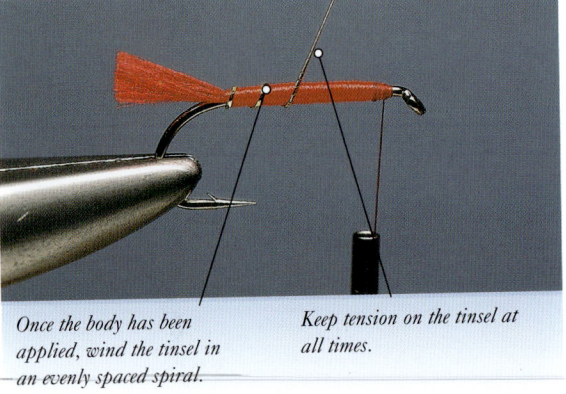

Once the body has been applied, wind the tinsel in an evenly spaced spiral.

Keep tension on the tinsel at all times.

4 Remove any waste ends of the tinsel and tail material that project over the eye before winding on the body. Take the tinsel and wind it over the body in open, evenly spaced turns.

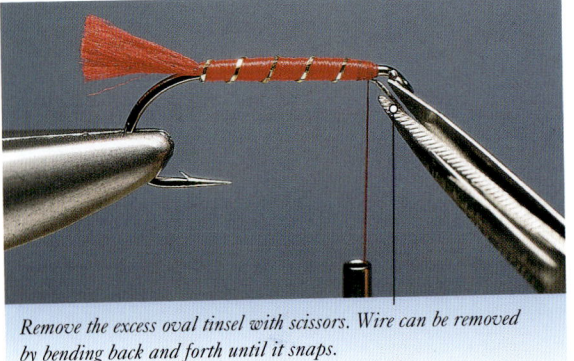

Remove the excess oval tinsel with scissors. Wire can be removed by bending back and forth until it snaps.

5 Apply five or six turns until the eye has been reached. Secure the loose end of the tinsel with the tying thread before using scissors to remove the excess.

CORE TECHNIQUE 4

Feather Fiber Body

Feather fiber is used widely in fly tying for the bodies of dry flies or nymphs. The delicate fibers are used to produce a slim, slightly tapering profile, ideal for mimicking the body of a small aquatic insect such as a mayfly or caddis fly. Various types of feather fiber may be used, the most common coming from the tail of a male ring-necked pheasant, or from the plumage of a goose. These may be either natural colors as in the chestnut brown of the Pheasant Tail Nymph or dyed various natural or gaudy colors. Because these fibers are very delicate they need to be protected in some way and the usual methods are to add a rib of some sort or to wind the fibers over a layer of wet lacquer.

1 Run the tying thread down to the hook bend in close turns. Catch in 2-inch (5-cm) fine nylon monofilament or wire, as a rib, then select five or six feather fibers.

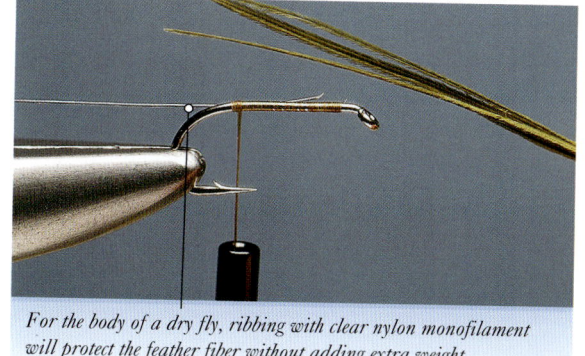

For the body of a dry fly, ribbing with clear nylon monofilament will protect the feather fiber without adding extra weight.

2 Check to ensure that all the fibers are undamaged and that the tips are level. Replace any that are not. Catch in the fibers, by their tips, at the hook bend.

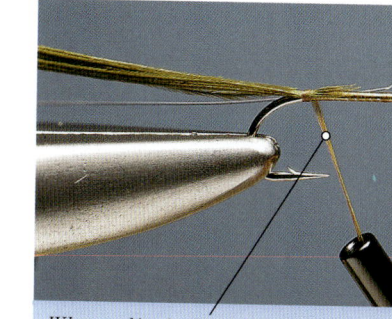

When catching in the feather fiber counterwind the thread so that it flattens and prevents an unsightly lump from forming.

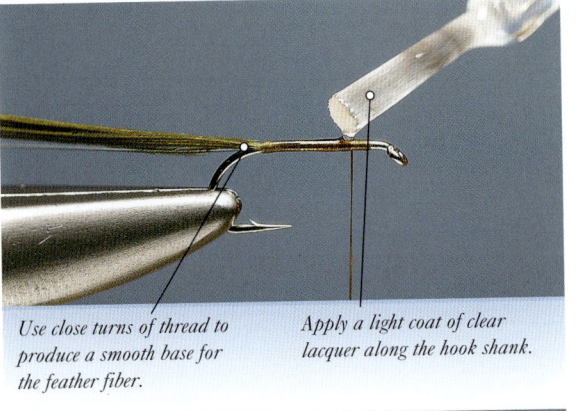

Use close turns of thread to produce a smooth base for the feather fiber.

Apply a light coat of clear lacquer along the hook shank.

3 Carry the tying thread back up the shank in close turns, securing the tips of feather and the waste end of the rib in place. Apply a thin coat of clear lacquer to the thread turns.

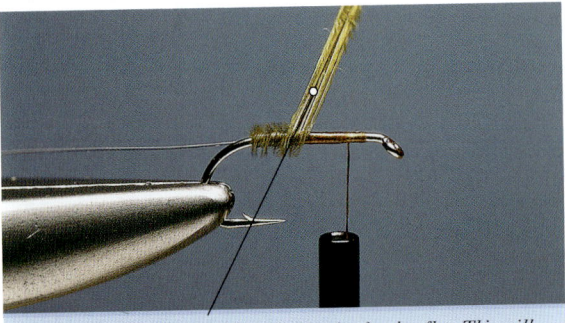

Ensure that the strands of fiber don't twist, but lay flat. This will produce a neat, tapered feather fiber effect.

4 Allow the lacquer a few seconds to become tacky, then wind the fibers along the shank in touching turns. Do not twist the fibers; instead, allow them to lay flat. This will produce the correct tapered profile.

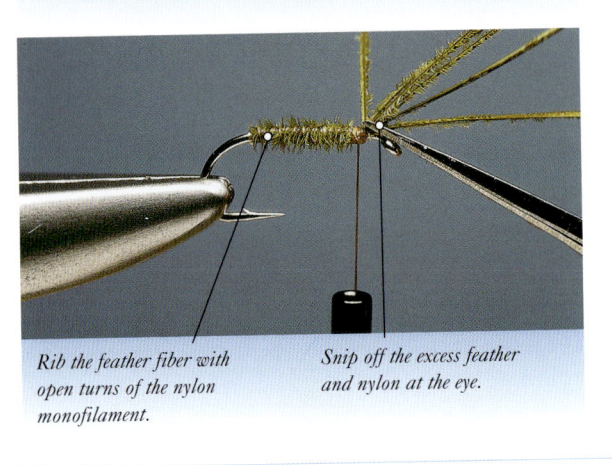

Rib the feather fiber with open turns of the nylon monofilament.

Snip off the excess feather and nylon at the eye.

5 When the fibers have been wound to a point just short of the eye, secure the loose ends with thread. Apply the rib in evenly spaced turns, securing the loose end and removing the excess.

CORE TECHNIQUE 5

Hairwing

The hair of many different animals is used in fly tying, from goat and squirrel to bear, arctic fox, and the tail of the white-tailed deer known to the fly tier as bucktail. Hair is generally very tough, and smooth, which makes it difficult to tie it in firmly. To solve the problem the thread must be strong enough to apply plenty of pressure but not so thick that too few turns can be made before the head becomes bulky. Here an 8/0 denier thread is perfect for most trout and salmon patterns. Locking turns of thread should be applied around the wing base. These not only help to secure the hair, but also control its shape and keep it in position. Finally, apply a drop of lacquer to the butts.

1 Complete the body so that the thread is positioned a short distance back from the eye. Select a slim bunch of hair, removing any underfur or damaged fibers.

Remove any damaged hairs including any that stick out.

Position the tying thread at the front of the body.

2 Making sure that the tips are roughly level, position the hair with two or three thread turns. Any hairs that don't sit correctly or are not level may be removed at this point.

Make the first positioning turns of thread halfway between the body and the hook eye.

Bed the locking turns of thread close to the first, positioning turns so that they are not visible when the head of the fly is completed.

3 Lift the wing and wind on two or three turns of thread directly around the base of the hair bunch.

Angle the scissors against the eye of the hook so that the cut puts a taper in the hair base (butts).

4 Continue winding the thread in the normal way, locking the hair to the hook. Apply plenty of pressure at this point. Trim away any excess hair using scissors.

Applying a drop of lacquer before the head of the fly is complete helps it to soak well into the hair.

5 Run a small amount of clear lacquer into the thread turns to help keep the hair in place. Finally, build a tidy head and cast off the thread with a whip finish.

CORE TECHNIQUE 6

Dubbing (Simple)

The standard method for producing a translucent fur body is known as dubbing. It is used in most types of flies from large, hairwing patterns right down to the smallest, delicate nymph or dry fly. In its simplest form, a dubbed body is created using a twisting action between finger and thumb so that the fur sticks to the thread. The end product is a fine, tapered yarn, which is then wound along the hook shank to form the body or thorax of the fly. The amount of fur applied affects the profile with the thickest, most dense types used mostly on larger patterns. To help the fur adhere to the thread, a light coat of wax may be applied first. This can be plain beeswax or a specially-made product.

1 Having wound the tying thread in close turns along the hook and caught in any tail or ribbing material, apply a light coating of wax to 3 to 4 inches (7.5–10 cm) of the thread.

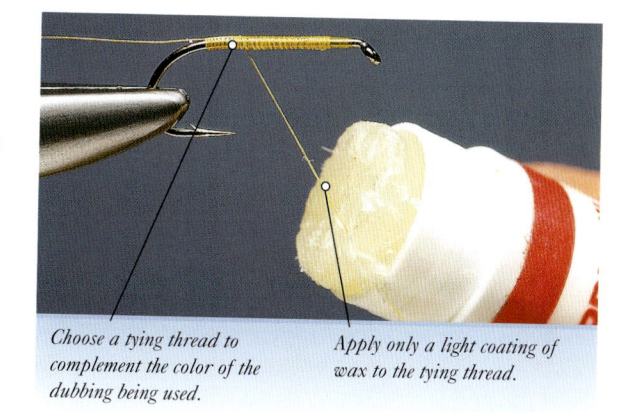

Choose a tying thread to complement the color of the dubbing being used.

Apply only a light coating of wax to the tying thread.

2 Take a pinch of the chosen fur and tease it out so that the direction of all the fibers is well mixed. Apply a small amount of the fur to the tying thread, spreading it out evenly.

The dubbing fur should be well teased out, to enable a light and even application to the thread.

Don't apply too much fur at one time.

Using light but definite pressure between finger and thumb twist the fur so that it creates a tapered rope around the thread. Always twist the fur in the same direction.

3 Between finger and thumb, begin to twist the fur and the thread together. Continue, always in the same direction, until a dense, tapered rope has been formed.

Make the first turn of the dubbed rope at the same point that the ribbing material was caught in.

4 Wind the dubbed fur rope back until it is at a position opposite the hook barb. From this point, wind the dubbed fur along the shank.

The rib should be wound once the body has been applied.

Make sure that the turns of dubbing sit closely together. This will produce a body with the correct density and no gaps.

5 Continue winding the dubbed fur in close turns until it is just short of the hook eye. Now the ribbing can be wound and any additional materials applied.

Dubbing Loop

This method works particularly well on small-to medium-sized patterns where the body needs to be delicate rather than having the bulk of some lure and wet fly patterns.

Using a dubbing loop produces a tighter, more precise effect than the standard finger-and-thumb twist. Because of this it works well where a slim tapered body is required that is not going to be teased out. There are various methods for creating a dubbing loop, including applying the fur into a preformed loop. The principle of the dubbing loop is that the dubbing material is applied, usually into a loop of tying thread, which is then twisted until it grips and binds the material to form a tight yarn.

1 Add any necessary tail material and position the thread a short distance from the bend. Take a small pinch of fine dubbing fur and, after ensuring that the fur is evenly spread, gently twist it onto the prewaxed thread.

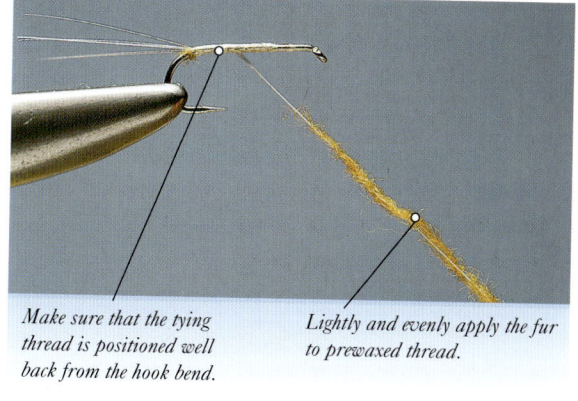

Make sure that the tying thread is positioned well back from the hook bend.

Lightly and evenly apply the fur to prewaxed thread.

2 Loop the thread around the arms of the dubbing twister, then back up to the hook. Wind on a few turns of thread to complete the loop, then take the main thread back up toward the eye.

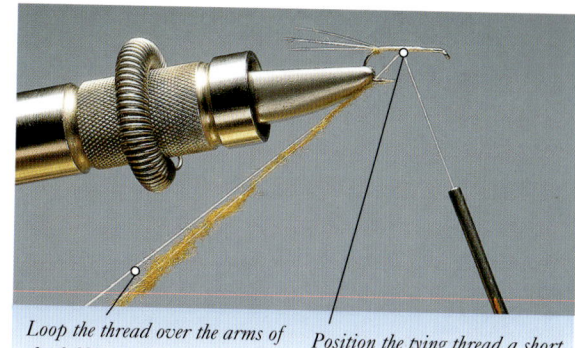

Loop the thread over the arms of the dubbing twister, then wind it back onto the hook to form a loop.

Position the tying thread a short distance from the hook eye.

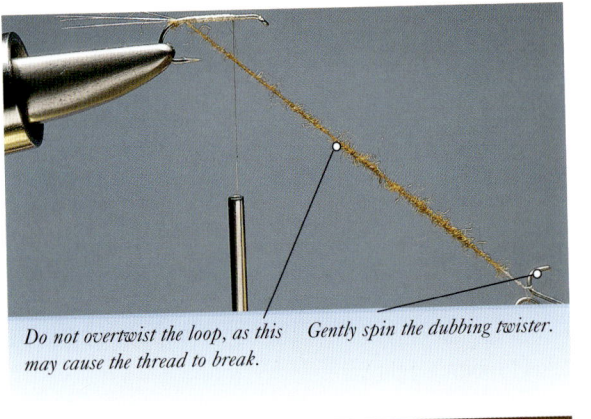

Do not overtwist the loop, as this may cause the thread to break.   *Gently spin the dubbing twister.*

3 Now spin the dubbing twister. This will cause the loop to close and the thread to wrap itself around the fibers of the dubbing material. Continue until a tight, thin yarn has been produced.

Begin applying the dubbing loop at the base of the tail.   *Keep the turns close so no gaps form.*

4 Again, maintaining tension on the thread with the dubbing twister, wind the yarn in close turns from the base of the tail. Make sure that no gaps form.

Use the dubbing twister to retain tension on the loop until its loose end has been firmly fixed with tying thread.

5 Continue winding the dubbing until two-thirds of the hook shank is covered. Secure the end of the loop with tying thread and remove any excess.

CORE TECHNIQUE 8

Hackletip Wing

Hackletips are used for wings in a large range of, mostly, dry fly patterns and, notably, in the most widely used dry fly of all—the Adams. Their shape lends them to a variety of imitative and more general patterns and they may be used to suggest the wings of mayflies, caddis flies, and midges along with a number of imitation terrestrials. Hackletips can be applied in different profiles from low and flat in the case of caddis fly or spinner wings to upright and set apart in the standard dry fly method. Both cock and hen hackles are used for this type of wing. Being wider and more rounded, the hen hackle is better suited to tying mayfly patterns, as the shape closely resembles that of the real insect's wings.

1 Having completed the body and tail of the fly, position the tying thread one-half of the body length back from the eye. Select two small gray hen hackles of equal size.

For small mayflies, the wider, rounded hen hackle is better suited than the slim cock hackle.

Make sure that the feathers are of equal size and shape.

2 Strip away the fibers from the base of both hackles to leave two tips of equal size. These should be approximately the same length as the hook.

Placing the hackles together when stripping the stem ensures that the remaining tips are of equal size.

Check the position of the wings after they have been caught in. They should project just past the hook bend.

3 Place them together face to face so the shinier backs of the feathers are on the outside. Catch them in, with two or three thread turns, just in front of the body.

Drawing the stripped stems between the two wings will help them separate and prevent them from pulling out.

4 Lift the feathers into a more upright position and fix with turns of thread. Next, draw the hackle stems between the feathers and, again, fix with further thread turns.

Use further wraps of thread to secure the wings in an upright position.

The thread is now positioned behind the wings ready to attach the hackle.

5 Remove the excess hackle stems with scissors, then position the wings by winding on another couple of thread turns between them and the body.

Weighted Underbody

Some flies that are designed to sink rely simply on the weight of the hook to help them cut through the water's surface. However, when a pattern needs to sink quickly, either in deep or fast-running water, it will require extra weight. This can be added in the form of metal beads or dumbbell eyes but when a lifelike profile needs to be maintained, the best solution is to use a weighted underbody. The beauty of the technique is that all the weight remains hidden beneath the material used for the body or thorax so that even a relatively slim nymph can incorporate additional weight; it means simply that the materials covering the underbody need to be as thin as possible.

1 Fix the hook securely in the vise, then take 3-inch (7.5-cm) medium-diameter lead wire and begin winding in on the shank a short distance from the bend.

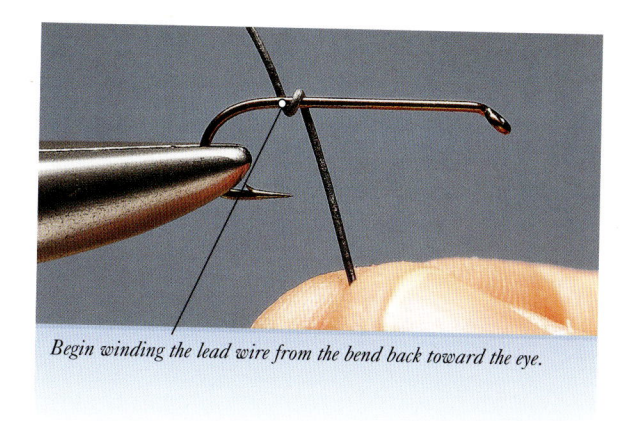

Begin winding the lead wire from the bend back toward the eye.

2 Continue winding the wire in close turns along the shank. Keep the turns closely butted together. If any gaps form, simply push the turns up close with the fingers.

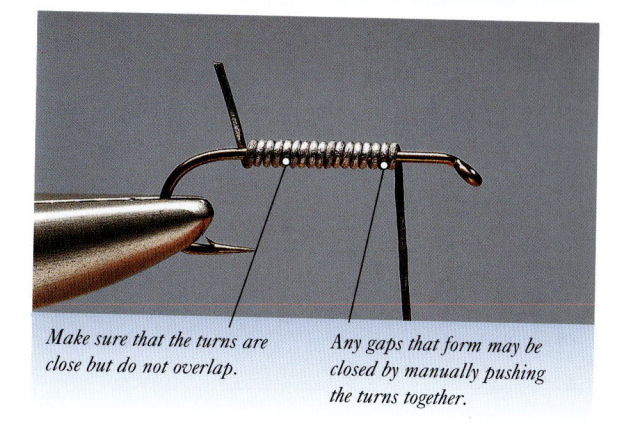

Make sure that the turns are close but do not overlap.

Any gaps that form may be closed by manually pushing the turns together.

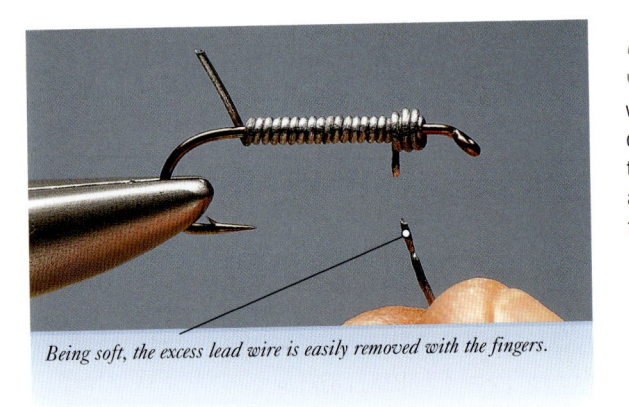

Being soft, the excess lead wire is easily removed with the fingers.

3 Once the wire has been taken almost to the eye, wind three or four turns back over themselves to form a thorax—or the wire may be left as a single layer. Simply wiggle the wire until the end breaks.

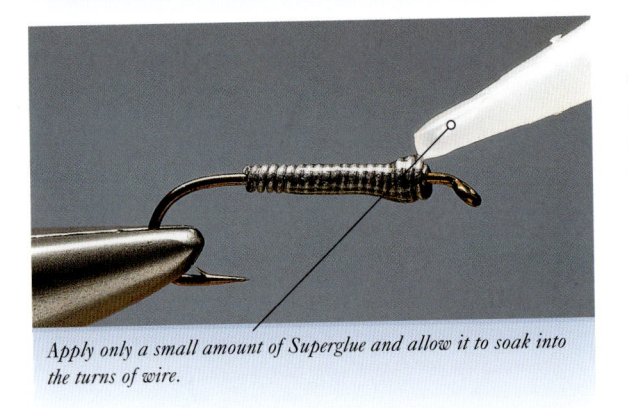

Apply only a small amount of Superglue and allow it to soak into the turns of wire.

4 Remove the waste end of wire at the tail end. Push the wire up so that a section of bare shank is left near the bend to accommodate the tail of the fly. Add a coat of super-strong adhesive.

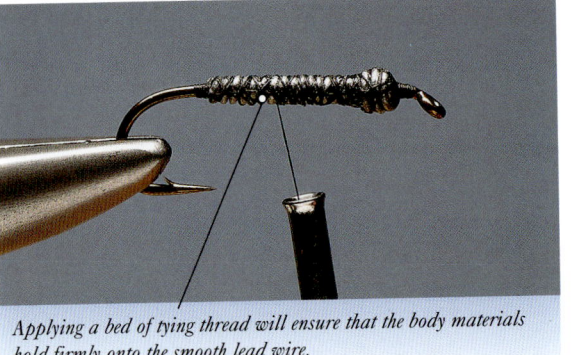

Applying a bed of tying thread will ensure that the body materials hold firmly onto the smooth lead wire.

5 When the glue has cured, cover the underbody in a layer of tying thread ready to accept the body and thorax materials.

CORE TECHNIQUE 10

Collar Hackle

The collar hackle forms the basis of so many trout and salmon fly patterns that it is, without a doubt, the ultimate core technique. In essence, the method used for producing a basic collar hackle is very simple, involving winding on a few turns of the appropriate feather just behind the eye of the hook. The main points to consider are the type of feather being used, its size, and remembering to leave enough room so that it doesn't end up right over the eye. First, always make sure that for a standard three- or four-turn hackle there is approximately one-quarter of the shank left free between the body and the eye. This should have a thin layer of tying thread covering it but no body materials.

1 With the body and tail in place, the thread should sit just in front of the body. Choose a hackle with the correct fiber length. This can be judged more easily by bending the hackle stem to flare the fibers.

Make sure that there is enough space between the body and the eye to accommodate the hackle.

Choose a hackle with fiber length about one-and-a-half to two times the hook gape.

2 Check the hackle to make sure that all the fibers are perfect, then gently tear the fibers away from around the base to leave a length of bare stem.

Gently tear away the soft fibers at the base of the hackle to leave a section of bare stem.

Catch in the hackle so that it is shiny side out.

Trim the stem to leave a short stub.

3 Trim this section of bare stem to leave a short stub and catch the hackle in by using two or three tight thread turns. Using the thin, bare stem section keeps bulk to a minimum.

Wind the hackle toward the eye in close turns.

Apply light tension with the hackle pliers at all times.

4 Take hold of the hackle by its tip, using a pair a specially designed hackle pliers. Make the first hackle turn just in front of the body, then apply a second, winding it toward the hook eye.

Fix the hackletip at the eye with tying thread.

When using scissors, take care to only remove the excess hackletip.

5 Add a further one or two turns, always working forward so that they do not overlap. Secure the loose hackletip with tight thread turns. Finally, remove the excess tip with sharp, fine-pointed scissors.

CORE TECHNIQUE 11

Spinning Deer Hair

Using deer body hair to create a large buoyant head is a technique employed in a range of surface and subsurface patterns. It involves spinning the hair around the hook shank and then trimming it to the desired shape, which depends on how the finished fly is going to be fished. Though deer hair is used to produce buoyant bodies on imitations of grasshoppers, caddis flies, plus fry, mice, and frogs, it was originally used as the head of the muddler minnow, a pattern designed to imitate a small bottom-dwelling fish similar to the miller's thumb or bullhead. Although the profile of all these patterns can be very different, all take advantage of the fact that deer hair is hollow and buoyant.

1 Having completed the body and wing of the fly form a smooth bed of tying thread between the wing and the hook eye. With the tips roughly level, catch in the hair with two loose thread turns so the tips project back over the wing.

Position the hair with two or three loose turns of thread. This would normally be achieved with the fingers holding the hair in place.

2 Now begin to draw the thread tight. As this happens the thread will pull into the hair and begin to drag or "spin" it around the hook. Apply further tight thread turns and, if necessary, use your fingers to ease the hair evenly around the hook.

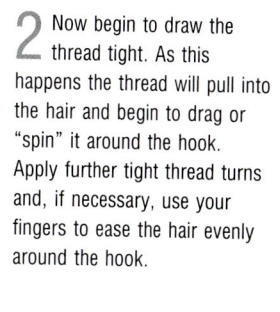

Drawing the thread tight will cause the hair to flare.

If necessary, ease the hair around the hook with the fingers.

3 Add more turns of thread, then draw the hair back and fix it firmly in place by adding yet more thread turns in front of it. This is very important as it will prevent the finished head from coming loose.

When the hair is distributed evenly around the hook fix in place with tight thread turns.

Stroke the hair back and apply more thread to fix.

4 Add a second bunch of deer hair in the same way as the first. With this second bunch, the fine tips may be removed first. Either way, make sure that this bunch is pushed firmly back against the first.

Continue adding small bunches of hair, filling the gap between the eye and the wing base.

Remove the tips of the hair for this section.

5 If there is room add another bunch of hair until the gap up to the eye has been filled. Push the hair back firmly so that it is compacted, then cast off the thread with a whip finish. Finally, trim the hair to shape.

Trim to a teardrop shape, taking care not to remove the hair tips which are left as a hackle.

Draw the hair back and cast off the thread with a whip finish.

CORE TECHNIQUE 12

Paired Wing— Soft Loop

This is the standard method for winging many wet fly patterns. In order to create the paired effect, slips are removed from opposing quills from a bird's wings. The most widely used materials are the gray wing feathers of duck species such as mallard and teal, but those of the starling are also used as a substitute for the blackbird and dotterel (a type of plover) where using the real thing is now prohibited. Game birds such as grouse, woodcock, and hen pheasant are also used where the mottled browns of their plumage reflect the hues of caddis fly wings, and those of large, dark mayfly species such as the March Brown. Whichever bird species is used, the procedure is the same.

1 Take one feather and, using a sharp implement such as scissor points, divide the webbing that joins the feather fibers to produce a thin slip.

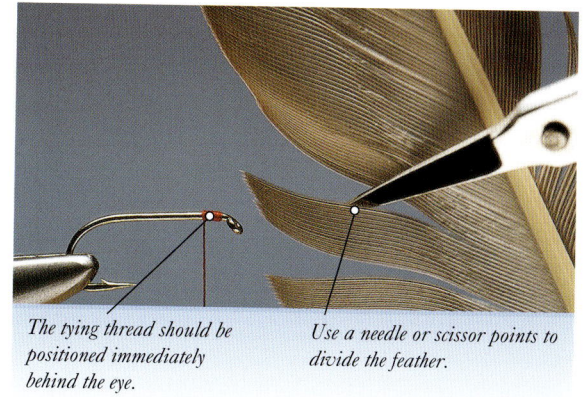

The tying thread should be positioned immediately behind the eye.

Use a needle or scissor points to divide the feather.

2 Repeat the process with a second feather. The aim is to create two slips of identical width. If one is greater simply remove the excess fibers.

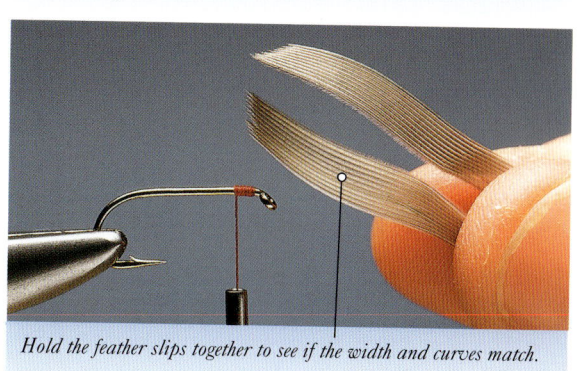

Hold the feather slips together to see if the width and curves match.

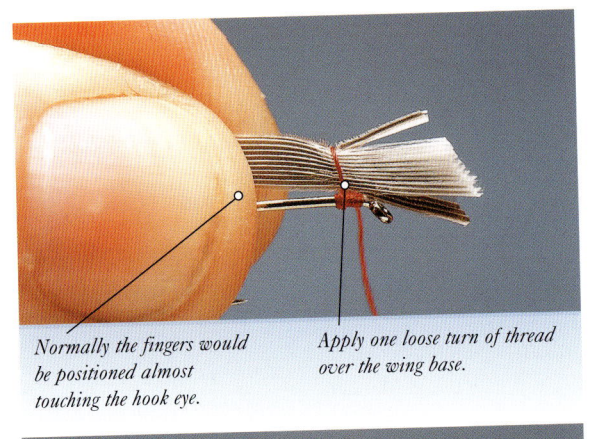

Normally the fingers would be positioned almost touching the hook eye.

Apply one loose turn of thread over the wing base.

3 Place the slips together so the tips are level and position the wing on top of the hook. Holding it in position, apply a single loose turn of thread. This is known as a "soft" or winging loop.

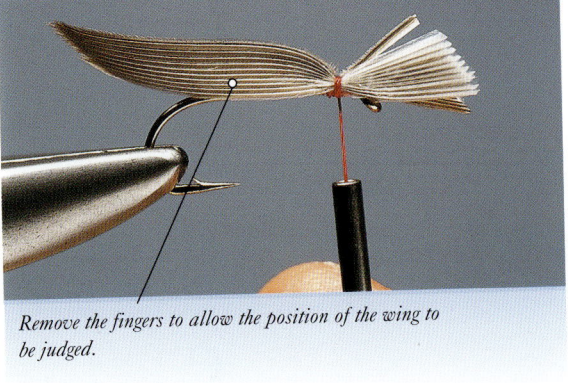

Remove the fingers to allow the position of the wing to be judged.

4 Carry the thread around the far side of the wing until it is positioned directly below the hook. Only now, apply tension so that the thread draws down, locking the wing in position.

Apply a few more thread turns to fix the wing in place.

Remove the excess with scissors angled with the eye.

5 Assuming that the wing is now sitting perfectly straight, apply another one or two "soft" loops, then further normal thread turns to secure the wing firmly in place. Finally, trim off any excess feather.

Tinsel Body

Using flat tinsel is a good way to make a smooth, sparkling body of the type used on many wet fly and streamer patterns.

Originally this tinsel was made from real metal, and it is still possible to obtain the genuine article, though the advantages of modern plastic alternatives outweigh those of metal. Although metal is tough, it tarnishes easily so that the wonderful sparkle created when the fly was first tied soon fades to a dull, lifeless finish. Plastic tinsels such as Mylar are nearly as tough and easier to apply, and are not prone to tarnishing.

1 Fix the hook in the vise and, before applying the tinsel body, catch in any tail and ribbing materials. Build a smooth base for the tinsel by covering the waste ends of any tail or rib with close turns of thread.

Cover waste ends of previous materials to form an even base.

Let waste ends of tail and rib lie along the hook shank.

2 Carry the tying thread along the shank, stopping just short of the eye. Cut a length of flat silver tinsel to a point and catch it in with tying thread.

Cutting the end of the tinsel to a point helps it to bend more easily when the first wrap is made.

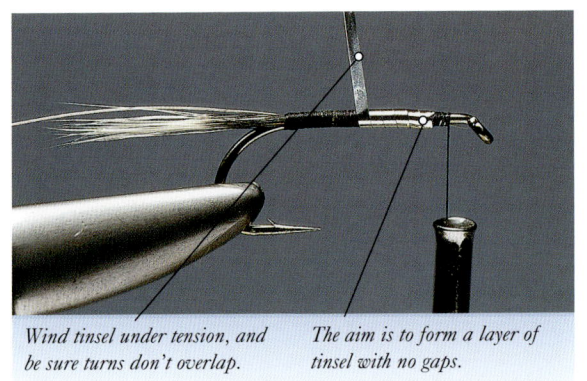

3 Take hold of the tinsel with your fingers and begin winding it down the hook shank. Ensure that the turns are butted closely together. If a gap does form, simply unwind the turn and reapply.

Wind tinsel under tension, and be sure turns don't overlap.

The aim is to form a layer of tinsel with no gaps.

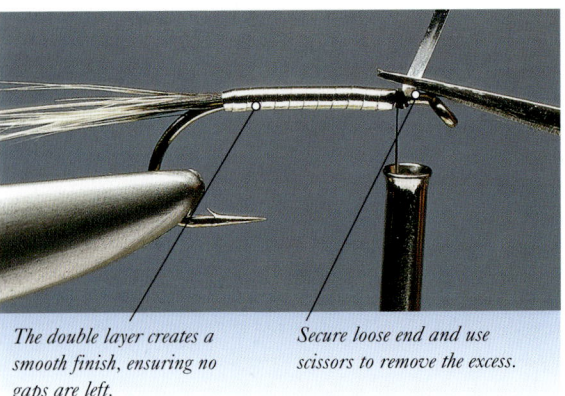

4 Keep winding the tinsel in close turns until you reach the base of the tail. Once you get to this point start winding the tinsel back over itself.

Don't allow tinsel to slip over base of the tail—stop it just short.

This procedure forms the first of the two layers.

5 Wind the tinsel back up the shank, toward the place where it was first caught in. Continue winding it right up to a point just short of the eye and secure the loose end.

The double layer creates a smooth finish, ensuring no gaps are left.

Secure loose end and use scissors to remove the excess.

CORE TECHNIQUE 14

Floss Body

Floss bodies are used in a wide number of fly patterns particularly in salmon flies, streamers, and a variety of traditional wet flies. The two most commonly used types of floss are made from rayon or natural silk. Being man-made, rayon doesn't deteriorate like silk and is also very smooth, creating a nice finish to the body. However, the fibers are prone to snagging when being applied, so it is a good idea to use a bobbin holder when winding—a procedure that also keeps waste to a minimum. Some types of floss comprise a number of strands twisted together. In order for them to be wound smoothly these either need to be divided before being caught in or counter-twisted as they are wound.

1 Run on the tying thread and catch in the ribbing material at the bend. Thread the floss through a large-diameter spigot bobbin holder.

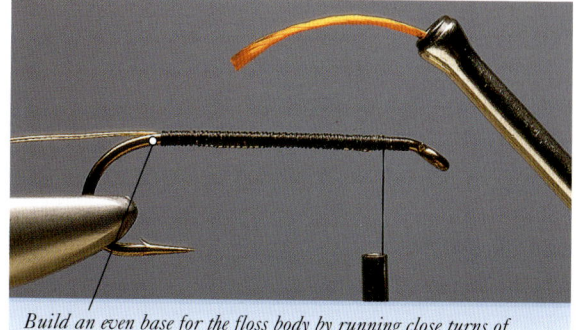

Build an even base for the floss body by running close turns of tying thread over the waste end of the tinsel and hook.

2 With the waste end of the ribbing material secured along the shank, catch in the floss with tying thread a short distance back from the eye.

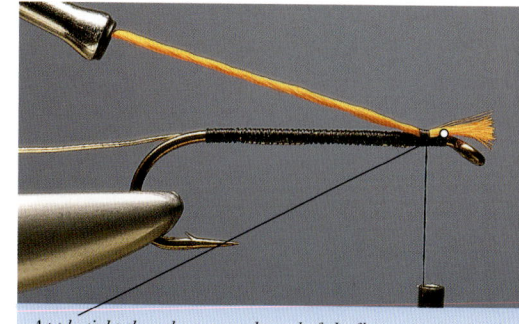

Apply tight thread turns to the end of the floss to secure it while being wound.

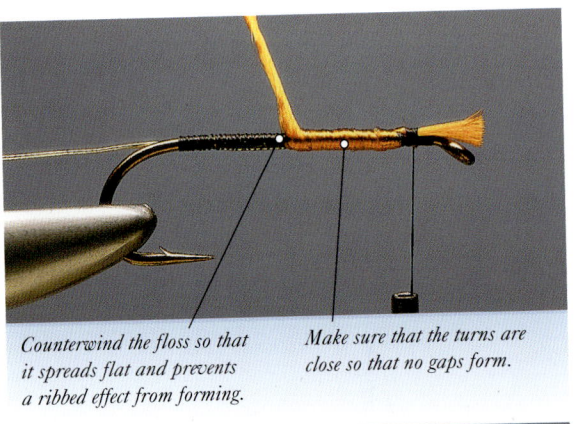

3 Begin to wind the floss down the shank toward the hook bend. Countertwisting the floss will help the fibers to lie flat and create a smooth effect.

Counterwind the floss so that it spreads flat and prevents a ribbed effect from forming.

Make sure that the turns are close so that no gaps form.

4 When the bend is reached, wind the floss back over the first layer. Make sure that the turns are touching so that no gaps form. If any do so, unwind the floss back to that point and reapply.

Applying a double layer of floss will help create a smooth effect.

Allowing the turns of floss to overlap slightly will taper the body.

5 When the floss has reached its catching-in point, secure the loose end with the tying thread. Apply the ribbing in open, evenly spaced turns and secure that too. Finally, remove the waste ends of the floss and ribbing.

When the loose end of the floss has been secured with tying thread, apply the rib in evenly spaced turns.

FLY
DIRECTORY

All of the major fly
groups are represented
in this book, from
nymphs and bugs and
wet flies to dry flies,
streamers, and hairwings.
Use the following fly
selector, which shows
you all 50 at a glance,
to choose the fly you
want to tie.

Fly Selector

Sparklewinged Spinner *110*

Orange Hopper *134*

Golden Olive Bumble *158*

Soldier Palmer *114*

Olive Midge Pupa *138*

March Brown *162*

Pale Morning Dun *118*

Sparkle Pupa *142*

Silver Invicta *166*

Blue-winged Olive *122*

Red Quill *146*

Fiery Brown *170*

CDC Greendrake *126*

GE Nymph *150*

Hot Butt Caddis *174*

Mayfly Cripple *130*

Baetis Nymph *154*

High-sight
Parachute Adams *178*

Royal Wulff 182	Tequila Flash 206	Blue Charm 230
X-Stimulator 186	Matuka 210	Rabbit Sculpin 234
Peeping Caddis 190	Conehead Bugger 214	Polar Fry 238
Crystal Cat 194	Minkie 218	Deer Hair Fry 242
Viva Booby 198	Egg-sucking Leech 222	Dave's Hopper 246
Ultra Clouser 202	Black Stonefly Nymph 226	

Hare's Ear Spider

Rather than imitating any specific insect or crustacean, the Hare's Ear Spider's versatility lies in the fact that it can be used to suggest several small aquatic food forms, such as a small mayfly nymph or caddis pupa.

It is a very easy pattern to tie though care must be taken when applying game bird feathers, such as partridge, as the thickness of the stem means that they are best caught in by their tip. The Hare's Ear Spider may be tied using only mottled brown hare's fur, or can be given an injection of color by applying a small thorax of red, orange, or lime green fur.

RECIPE

HOOK:	*Size 14–16 mediumweight wet fly*
THREAD:	*Brown*
RIB:	*Fine gold wire*
BODY:	*Hare's fur*
HACKLE:	*Brown partridge*
THORAX:	*Red, orange, lime green, or hare's fur*

1 Wind the tying thread along the hook shank until it has reached a point almost opposite the hook barb, then remove 2 inches (5 cm) of fine gold wire from the spool and catch it in so it sits on the far side of the hook.

FISH FOR:

Brown trout

Grayling

Rainbow trout

2 Cover the waste end of the wire with close turns of thread. This has the dual purpose of securing the wire and creating an even base for the body. Offer a small pinch of hare's fur to the thread.

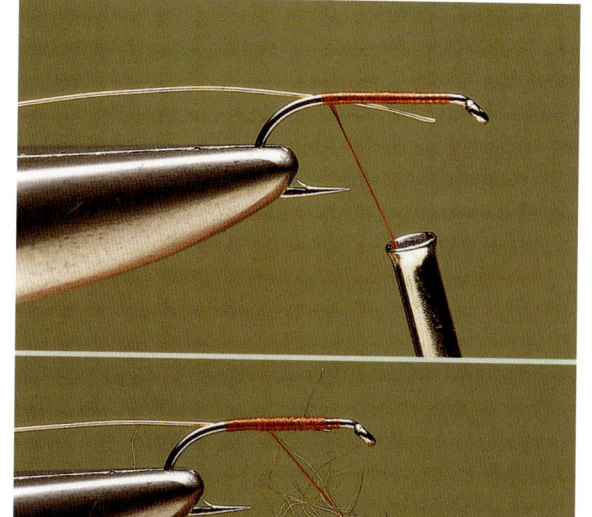

Hare's fur

With its mottle brown coloration hare's fur is a superb material for suggesting all manner of small aquatic creatures. Either the fur from the hare's body or alternatively from its mask and ears may be used to provide a range of effects.

Fine gold wire

The gold color of this wire makes the perfect complement to the mottled brown hues of both hare's fur and partridge feather. It also adds a touch of sparkle and strength to the body.

Brown partridge

This feather, taken from an English partridge, has a wonderfully fine mottling that combines so well with the similar hues of the hare's fur. It is also very mobile making it ideal for the hackle on many small spider patterns and wet flies.

Red fur

The thorax of the Hare's Ear Spider may be either plain hare's fur or a brighter, more visible color. Red works well but so too does orange or even fluorescent lime green. Tying the hackle tight up against the thorax lifts the fibers and gives them an extra kick.

3 Using a simple finger-and-thumb twist, dub the hare's fur into a thin rope. Adding a little wax to the thread first will help the fur adhere. Beginning at the wire's catching-in point, wind the fur along the hook shank.

4 Continue winding the dubbed hare's fur until three-quarters of the hook shank has been covered. That done, take hold of the wire and wind it over the body in five evenly spaced turns.

5 Secure the end of the wire with thread and remove the excess with scissors or by wiggling it until it breaks. Dub on a tiny pinch of red fur and apply as a thorax, leaving a small gap behind the eye.

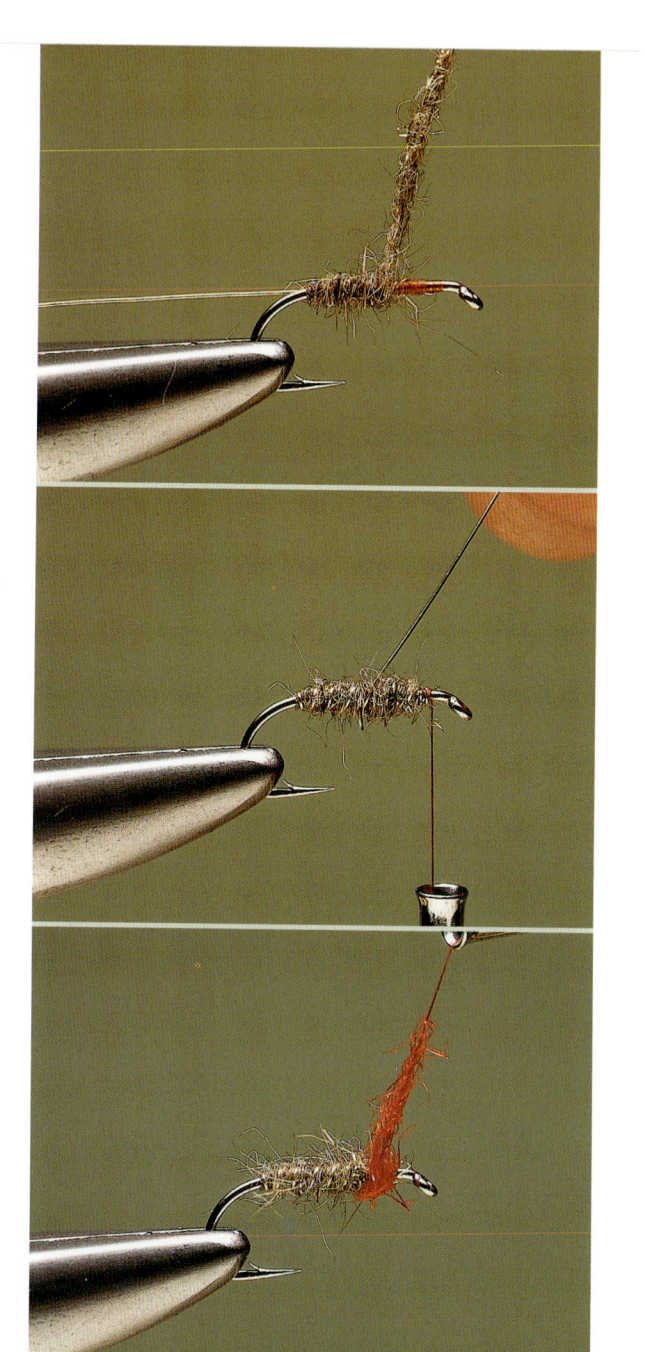

6 Take a small brown partridge feather. Stroke the fibers back to expose the very tip of the feather. Using two or three turns of the tying thread, catch the hackle in by this tip before removing the excess.

7 Holding the partridge hackle by its base, carefully wind on two turns. As each turn is made stroke the fibers back so they sit over the body.

8 Fix the hackle stem in place with thread before removing the excess. Build a small, neat head with tying thread before casting it off with a secure whip finish.

See also   DUBBING (SIMPLE), PAGE 28

COLLAR HACKLE, PAGE 36

Diawl Bach

RECIPE

HOOK:	*Size 10–14 wet fly*
THREAD:	*Black*
TAIL:	*Brown cock hackle fibers*
RIB:	*Medium-width copper wire*
BODY:	*Peacock herl*
HACKLE:	*Brown cock hackle fibers*
THORAX:	*Peacock herl*
CHEEKS:	*Red holographic tinsel*

It's been called magic on a hook, and the natural iridescence of peacock herl certainly makes it a tremendously effective material for tying all kinds of nymph, dry, and wet fly patterns.

In the case of the Diawl Bach, which is Welsh for Little Devil, it creates a slim, sparkling effect that in this particular version is enhanced by adding cheeks of red holographic tinsel.

Though peacock herl is easy to apply, its main drawback is susceptibility to damage. This can be alleviated by twisting the herls with the tying thread or ribbing them with a strong material such as copper wire.

1 Secure the hook in the vise and run on the tying thread at the eye. Wind it down the shank in close turns, stopping opposite the barb. There, catch in a few fibers of brown cock hackle.

FISH FOR:

Brown trout

Rainbow trout

2 Take 2 inches (5 cm) of medium-width copper wire and catch that in at the base of the tail. At the same point, catch in two fine strands of peacock herl by their tips.

Peacock herl
Aside from its iridescence, what is also great about peacock herl is that it can be used to give the impression of bulk without adding weight.

Holographic tinsel
This flat mylar tinsel has a holographic pattern that imparts a subtle sparkle to any pattern. It is available in a variety of colors including silver, blue, and red.

Copper wire
Copper wire is available in a variety of diameters and colors. Here, medium-width wire with a traditional reddish hue is used but others, such as green, may also be used to great effect.

Brown cock hackle fibers
A few brown cock hackle fibers are used both for the tail and hackle of the Diawl Bach. They are there to add a small degree of movement and to suggest the tails and legs of a nymph.

3 Using close turns of tying
thread, cover the waste
ends of all three materials. This
not only secures them firmly in
place but also creates a
smooth, even base on which to
apply the body.

4 With the tying thread
positioned two-thirds of the
way back to the eye, hold the
peacock herls and wind them
anticlockwise along the hook
shank to form a slim body.

5 Secure the loose ends of
the peacock herls when
they reach the tying thread but
do not remove them at this
point. Next, wind the copper
wire over the body in four or
five open, evenly spaced turns.

6 Secure the loose end of the wire with thread and remove the excess by cutting or wiggling it until it fatigues. Catch in a strand of red holographic tinsel on either side of the hook.

7 Take the loose ends of the peacock herls and wind them to form a short thorax. Secure the ends at the eye, remove, then draw the holographic tinsel on either side of the thorax and secure at the eye.

8 Remove the excess holographic tinsel, then catch in a few fibers of brown cock hackle underneath the hook. If necessary, invert the hook to achieve this. Finally, cast off with a whip finish.

See also   RIBBING SET, PAGE 22

FEATHER FIBER BODY, PAGE 24

Flashback Pheasant Tail Nymph

RECIPE

HOOK:	*Size 12–16 wet fly*
THREAD:	*Black*
TAIL:	*Cock pheasant tail fibers*
RIB:	*Fine copper wire*
BODY:	*Cock pheasant tail fibers*
WING CASE:	*Flat pearl tinsel*
THORAX:	*Peacock herl*

This is a great little pattern that is based on the original Pheasant Tail Nymph created by Frank Sawyer.

The key to its success is the sparkle created by adding flat pearl tinsel either as a thorax cover or along the entire length of the body. Both methods work, though the former adds just the right amount of flash to what is basically a fly of natural hues.

As pheasant tail fibers are prone to damage, they can be protected in various ways. One method includes winding them over a layer of wet lacquer; another is to add a protective rib of metal wire or nylon monofilament.

1 Run the tying thread on at the eye and carry it down to the bend in close turns. At a point opposite the hook barb catch in five or six fibers of cock pheasant tail allowing their tips to form the tail.

FISH FOR:

Brown trout

Cutthroat

Rainbow trout

2 With the tips of the pheasant tail fibers projecting back past the hook bend, take 2 inches (5 cm) of fine copper wire and catch it in at the same point.

Cock pheasant tail fibers
The rich chestnut-colored fibers found in the tail feather of the male ring-necked pheasant provide the body material for this classic pattern.

Pearl tinsel
Pearl tinsel adds a wonderful sparkle to any artificial fly. Here it is used as the thorax cover but having the tinsel running along the entire length of the body will increase the effect.

Copper wire
Ribbing the body with fine, copper wire adds both weight and some protection to the delicate pheasant tail fibers.

Peacock herl
The original Pheasant Tail nymph used strands of pheasant tail for the thorax. The Flashback version has even more impact by using the natural iridescence of peacock herl.

3 Carry the tying thread two-thirds of the way back up the shank, using the turns to fix the waste end of the wire along the shank. Take hold of the fibers and make a single wrap close to the tail base.

4 Don't twist the pheasant tail fibers but allow them to spread flat as they are wound. The result is an even body with a slight taper. To protect the delicate fibers, a coat of clear lacquer may first be applied to the thread base.

5 Once the turns of pheasant tail have covered two-thirds of the hook's length, secure the loose ends with turns of thread. Take hold of the wire and counterwind it over the pheasant tail fibers so that it crosses them.

6 Secure the end of the wire and remove the excess and that of the pheasant tail fibers. That done, catch in a strip of wide pearl tinsel plus two strands of peacock herl just in front of the body.

7 Take the tying thread up to the eye, then, holding the ends of the peacock herls, wind them without twisting to form the thorax.

8 Secure and remove the ends of the peacock herls before drawing the pearl tinsel over the back of the thorax. Secure that too at the eye and remove the excess. Build a neat head and cast off with a whip finish.

See also   RIBBING SET, PAGE 22

FEATHER FIBER BODY, PAGE 24

Claret Emerger

This pattern was developed specifically to imitate a Chironomid midge pupa at the very point it transforms into the adult. The pearl rib does a great job in suggesting the sparkle created in the natural's body by trapped gasses, and the slim body mimics the profile of the Chironomid. Clipping away the hackle fibers beneath the hook ensures that the pattern sits very low in the surface film and is very important in making this pattern so successful.

Whereas the collar hackle helps the fly to float, teasing out the fibers of the body and thorax to increase the pattern's footprint on the water's surface enhances its effect.

RECIPE

HOOK:	*Size 12–14 light wire dry fly*
THREAD:	*Black*
RIB:	*Fine, flat pearl tinsel*
BODY:	*Claret seal's fur or substitute*
HACKLE:	*Brown cock hackle*
THORAX:	*Claret seal's fur or substitute*

1 Fix the hook in the vise and run the tying thread on at the eye. Carry the thread down the shank in touching turns until it has reached a point opposite the bend. There catch in 2 inches (5 cm) of fine pearl tinsel.

FISH FOR:

Brown trout

Rainbow trout

2 Secure the waste ends of the tinsel along the shank with open turns of thread. Add a light coat of wax to the tying thread before applying a small pinch of claret fur.

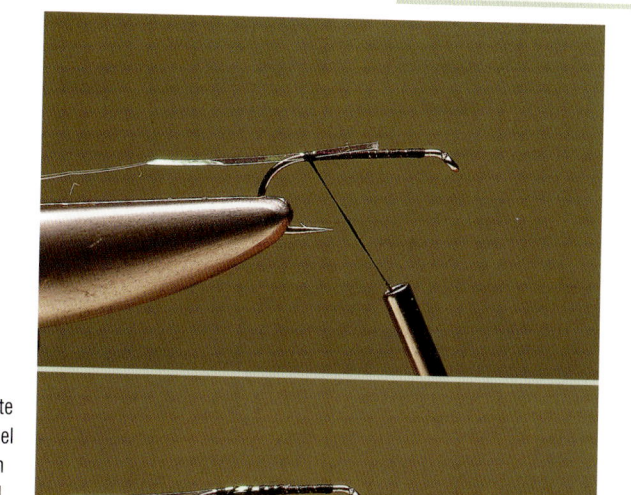

Brown cock hackles

A couple of turns of brown cock hackle help this fly to float and mimic the shades of the natural midge.

Fine pearl tinsel

The sparkle produced by pearl tinsel is ideal for mimicking that found in the body of a real emerging midge.

Claret fur

Claret fur gives a rich sparkle, ideal for imitating a small emerging midge. Teasing out the fur with a needle or a piece of Velcro suggests the legs of the emerging insect along with imparting translucency.

3 Using a simple finger-and-thumb twist, dub the fur onto the tying thread to form a slim, tapered rope. Starting from where the tinsel was caught in, wind the fur along the hook in close turns.

4 Continue winding the dubbed fur until it has covered two-thirds of the hook shank. Next, take hold of the pearl tinsel and wind it in evenly spaced turns over the body. Between five and six turns is ample.

5 Secure the loose end of the tinsel with tying thread and remove the excess. Take a second, smaller pinch of claret fur and apply it to the tying thread in the same manner as the first.

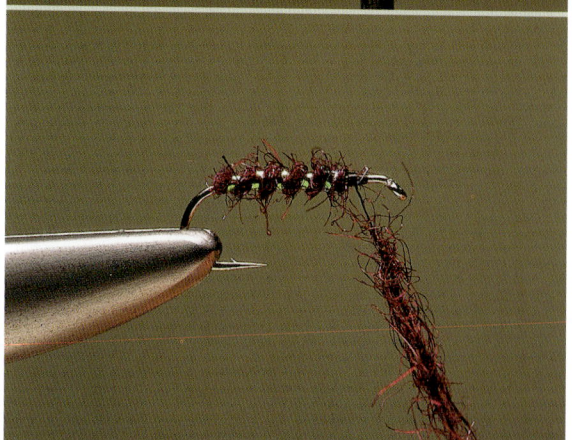

6 Starting right at the front of the body, wind on turns of the dubbed fur to create a small but pronounced thorax. Stop a short way from the eye to leave room for the hackle.

7 Prepare a brown cock hackle, choosing one with fibers around twice the length of the hook gape. Catch it in by its base and, using hackle pliers, wind on three full turns.

8 Secure the loose tip of the hackle with tying thread and remove the excess feather. Build a small, neat head, casting off the thread with a whip finish. Finally, trim away the hackle fibers beneath the hook.

See also   DUBBING (SIMPLE), PAGE 28

COLLAR HACKLE, PAGE 36

QE Damselfly Nymph

RECIPE

HOOK:	*Size 10 Living Nymph hook*
THREAD:	*Olive*
EYES:	*Green glass beads*
WEIGHT:	*Lead wire (optional)*
TAIL:	*Dyed olive marabou*
RIB:	*Chartreuse or olive wire*
BODY:	*Dyed olive marabou*
HACKLE & THORAX:	*Dyed olive marabou*

QE stands for "quick and easy," and that's just what this pattern is. Natural damselfly nymphs have a lot of movement, wiggling their abdomens from side to side in a sinuous, lashing motion. This is best imitated by using a soft, highly mobile material such as marabou.

The QE Damselfly Nymph uses dyed olive marabou for both the tail and hackle to inject as much movement as possible. The same material is also used for the body and thorax. The other key factor of this large but delicate nymph is to keep the overall effect nice and slim—just like the real thing. Either way it uses the technique of paired feather slips to form the wing.

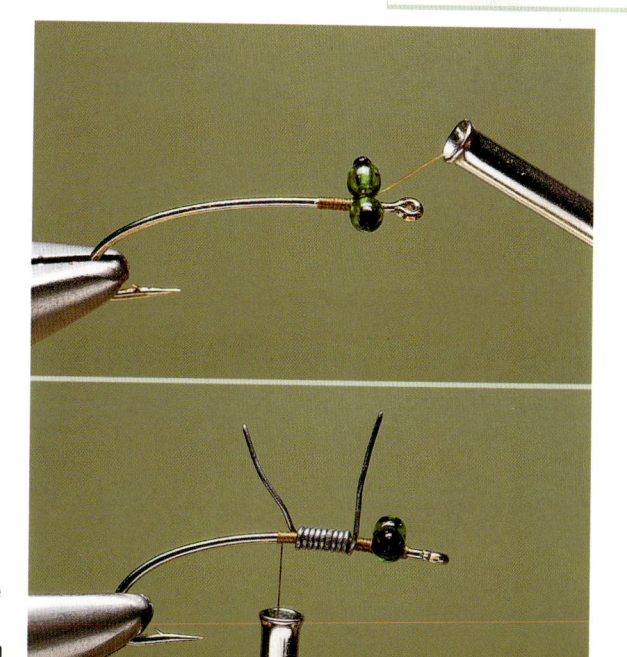

1 Having fixed the hook securely in the vise, run on a bed of tying thread just behind the eye. Catch in a pair of glass eyes connected by nylon monofilament melted at either end.

FISH FOR:

Brown trout

Rainbow trout

Cutthroat

2 Fix the eyes in position with figure-of-eight thread turns. Carry the thread halfway down the hook before covering it with close turns of lead wire wound in the position of the thorax.

Lead wire
Fine lead wire is a quick and easy way of adding weight to any fly.

Chartreuse wire
Copper wire is now available in a wide range of colors, making it very useful for ribbing all sorts of flies. In this pattern chartreuse or olive wire complements and protects the olive marabou while suggesting segmentation.

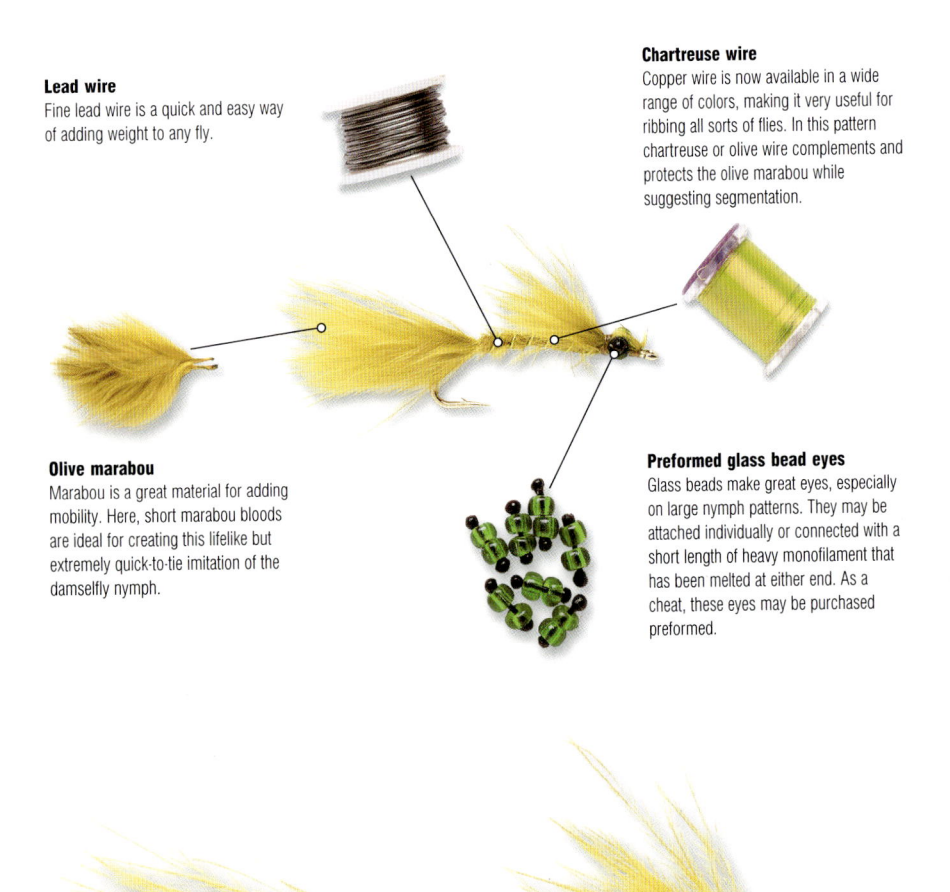

Olive marabou
Marabou is a great material for adding mobility. Here, short marabou bloods are ideal for creating this lifelike but extremely quick-to-tie imitation of the damselfly nymph.

Preformed glass bead eyes
Glass beads make great eyes, especially on large nymph patterns. They may be attached individually or connected with a short length of heavy monofilament that has been melted at either end. As a cheat, these eyes may be purchased preformed.

3 Remove the excess wire and fix the turns in place with the tying thread. Carry the thread down the shank in close turns until it begins to go around the bend of the hook.

4 Take a pinch of dyed olive marabou and catch it in with three tight turns, allowing the tips to project back to form the tail.

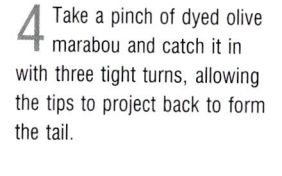

5 Secure the waste ends of marabou and remove the excess. Next, at the base of the tail catch in three or four strands of marabou by their tips plus 3 inches (7.5 cm) of the wire.

6 Cover the waste ends of the wire and marabou, carrying the thread up to the rear of the eyes. Holding the marabou gently, wind it up to the thread. Allow the strands to lay flat to form a slim body.

7 Wind the lead wire over the body in six evenly spaced turns before securing the loose end and removing the excess. Catch in another small bunch of marabou so that the tips project past the eye.

8 Wind the thread to the rear of the eyes, then draw the marabou back so the tips project over the top and sides of the body. Fix with thread, then cast off with a whip finish. Pinch off any stray fibers from tail and hackle.

See also   RIBBING SET, PAGE 22

WEIGHTED UNDERBODY, PAGE 34

Cruncher

The Cruncher is basically a variation on the Pheasant Tail theme, producing a hybrid wet fly/nymph that has proved very effective on a wide range of lakes and small stillwaters.

The original was tied using peacock herl for the thorax but its versatility can be increased by using different colors of fur, such as red, orange, or lime green. Either way, the important part of the fly is the way the thorax is formed so that the hackle will kick back against it, keeping the fibers in a more upright profile rather than allowing them to sweep back low over the body. This means that they create added movement when the fly is being retrieved.

RECIPE

HOOK:	*Size 8–14 wet fly*
THREAD:	*Brown*
TAIL:	*Honey-colored cock hackle fibers*
RIB:	*Fine silver wire*
BODY:	*Cock pheasant tail fibers*
HACKLE:	*Light-colored furnace hackle*
THORAX:	*Orange fur*

1 Fix the hook in the vise and run the tying thread down the shank in touching turns. Take a few fibers of honey-colored cock hackle and catch them in at a point opposite the barb.

FISH FOR:

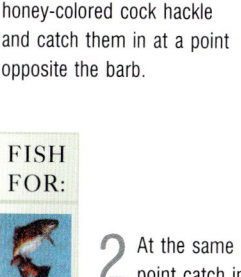

Brown trout

Rainbow trout

2 At the same point catch in 2 inches (5 cm) of fine silver wire, then take five cock pheasant tail fibers and catch them in by their tips, at exactly the same place.

Furnace hackles
When tying nymph/wet fly hybrids such as the Cruncher use either hen or soft-fibered cock hackles to impart plenty of movement into the fly. Here a furnace hackle is used—this has a dark center and light, honey-colored edges.

Orange dubbing
Ordinary peacock herl was used for the thorax in the original Cruncher, however, other materials also work well. Here orange fur has been used to inject a splash of color.

Light pheasant tail
Normally the rich chestnut-colored tails are sought out for tying patterns such as the Flashback Pheasant Tail Nymph. Here a paler colored feather produces a different but no less killing effect.

Honey cock hackles
Honey or pale ginger cock hackle fibers are used to suggest the shuck of a hatching nymph.

Silver wire
Fine silver wire adds a touch of sparkle to the body along with giving some protection to the delicate pheasant tail fibers.

3 Cover the waste ends of the hackle fibers, wire, and pheasant tail with close turns of tying thread. This will secure the materials in place and form an even base for the body.

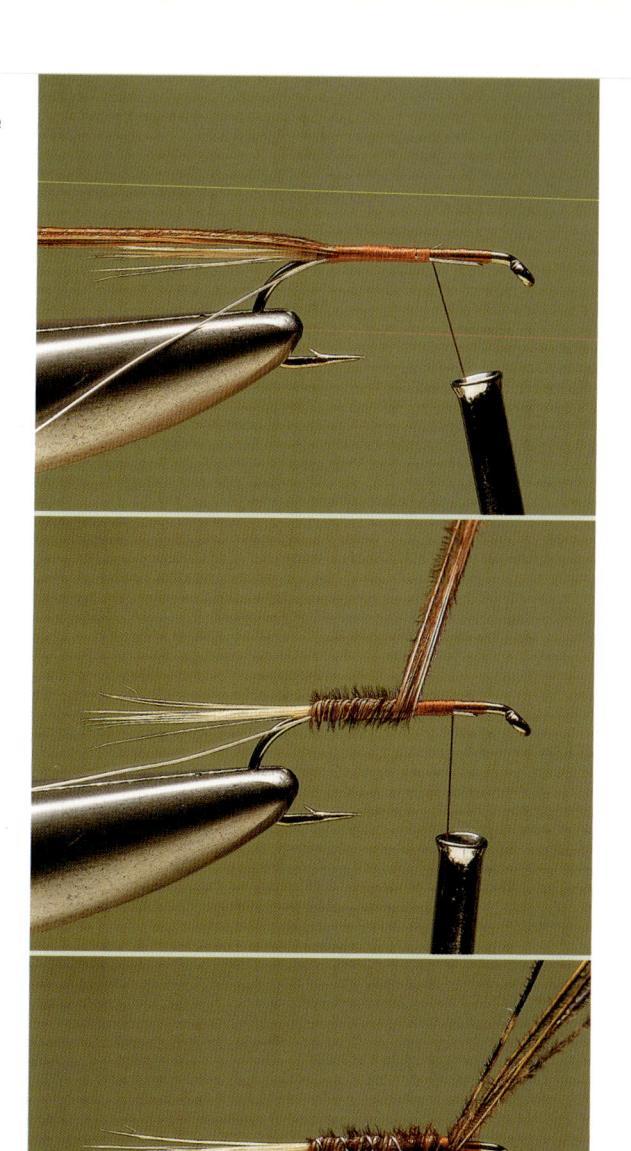

4 With the tying thread now positioned two-thirds of the way back toward the eye, wind the pheasant tail fibers along the shank. Do not twist them; instead, allow them to lie flat.

5 Once the fibers have reached the tying thread use it to secure the loose ends. Next, take the silver wire and wind on five turns in the opposite direction so the wire crosses the turns of pheasant tail.

6 With the rib in place secure the loose end of the wire with thread. Remove the waste ends with scissors. As an alternative, the wire can simply be snapped off to save blunting the scissors.

7 Take a small pinch of red fur and dub it onto the tying thread. Wind the dubbed fur in front of the body to form a short but pronounced thorax.

8 Take a light-colored furnace or Greenwell hackle. Prepare and attach it in the normal way before winding on three turns to form a collar. Complete the fly with a neat head and a whip finish.

See also   FEATHER FIBER BODY, PAGE 24

COLLAR HACKLE, PAGE 36

X-Beetle

Rubber-legged patterns work extremely well, the fine rubber strands kick up vibrations that attract all kinds of predatory fish, including trout. Even on small, imitative patterns, such as those tied to represent ants and beetles, the addition of rubber legs can make an already effective fly even better. Here, they are used to add movement to a black Foam Beetle—a fly that has proved its worth when trout are taking small, black terrestrials on either river or lake.

When using foam it is important not to stretch it or compress it with tying thread as this will drastically reduce its buoyancy.

RECIPE

HOOK:	*Size 12–16 mediumweight wet fly*
THREAD:	*Black*
BODY:	*Peacock Glister*
LEGS:	*Fine black, rubber strands*
WING CASES:	*Black microcellular foam*
THORAX:	*Peacock Glister or Ice Dub*
SIGHTER:	*Pink Glo Bug yarn*

1 Run on the tying thread, winding it down the hook shank in close turns to create a solid base for the other materials. Take it back up the shank and catch in a length of black foam dowel a short distance from the eye.

FISH FOR:

Brown trout

2 Secure the foam along the shank with open turns of thread. This prevents the foam from being crushed and its buoyancy reduced. At the bend secure the foam with further tight turns of thread.

Cutthroat

Rainbow trout

Black Foam
Microcellular foam comes in a number of forms including dowel and a thin sheet. Either will give this pattern the necessary buoyancy but the dowel needs less preparation.

Pink Glo Bug yarn
This fluorescent material comes in a range of colors and is ideal for adding visibility to patterns that sit very low in the water such as beetles, ants, and parachute flies.

Black rubber legs
These fine rubber strands add a real kick to any fly. For convenience they come in strip form where the individual strands are simply torn off when needed.

Peacock Ice Dub
This material and similar ones such as Glister produce a nice texture and sparkle ideal for beetle patterns.

3 Take a pinch of Peacock
Glister and apply it to the
tying thread. This material is not
easy to dub so you may need to
apply a coat of wax first. Dub
the Glister onto the thread and
wind the resulting rope along
the shank.

4 Continue winding the
dubbed rope in close turns
until two-thirds of the shank has
been covered and a chunky
body created. Draw, but do not
stretch, the foam over the back
of the body and secure with
tying thread.

5 Take a short section of
black rubber strand and
catch it in halfway along its
length with a couple of thread
wraps. This will create a V-
shape in the rubber and form
two distinct legs. Repeat the
process on the other side of
the body.

6 Remove a short length of pink or orange Glo Bug yarn and catch it in on top on the body with tight thread wraps. Pulling the thread tight at this stage will cause the yarn to flare.

7 Add a second, smaller pinch of the Glister and wind it up to the eye to form the thorax. Draw the remaining foam over the back of the thorax and secure at the eye with tying thread.

8 Cast off the tying thread with a whip finish, then trim the yarn sighter, the rubber legs, and finally the foam down to the correct length.

See also   DUBBING (SIMPLE), PAGE 28

Crystal Prince

The Goldhead Prince Nymph is surely one of the most popular general nymph patterns for catching game fish of all kinds on rivers and lakes. This pattern is simply a little twist on the theme, substituting strands of Krystal Flash for the white goose biot wing and thus adding even more sparkle.

The body comprises strands of peacock herl—a wonderfully iridescent, but fragile, material. Various methods including ribbing are used to protect the delicate herls. Another involves twisting the herl with the tying thread before it is wound. Wire can be used instead of the thread for an ultratough finish.

RECIPE

HOOK:	*Size 12–16 wet fly*
THREAD:	*Black*
TAIL:	*Brown goose biots*
RIB:	*Fine oval gold tinsel*
BODY:	*Peacock herl*
WING:	*Pearl Krystal Flash*
HACKLE:	*Brown cock hackle*
HEAD:	*Metal gold bead*

1 Slip on the gold bead before fixing the hook in the vise. Remember, too, that

FISH FOR:

the larger hole in the bead should be positioned to the rear. Wind on close turns of lead wire.

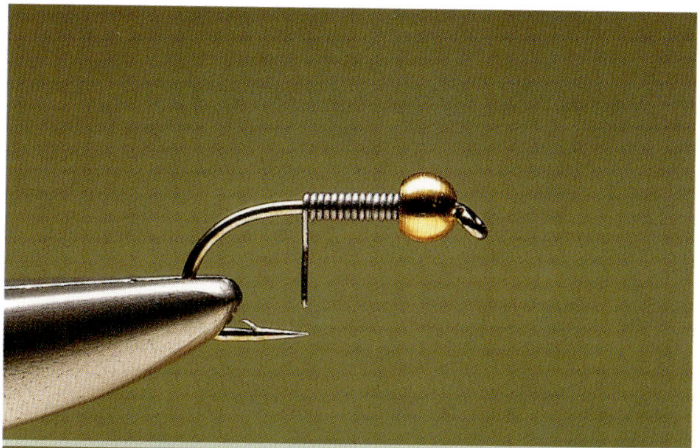

Brown trout

Cutthroat

2 Push the turns of wire so that a few sit in the recess in the back of the bead. Cover the remaining wire with turns of tying thread before catching in two brown goose biots at the hook bend.

Rainbow trout

Grayling

Brown goose biots
These spiky feathers come from the leading edge of the feather where the fibers are short and spiky. Being wide, with no flue they are perfect for tying the tails on general patterns such as the Prince nymph and the Crystal variant.

Pearl Krystal Flash
The tiny facets in this fine pearl tinsel produce a tremendous sparkle, changing color as they are turned in the light. The effect really does attract fish.

Gold beads
These metal beads come in a range of sizes and colors to suit any pattern. They also come in standard metal and superfast-sinking tungsten. Gold is the color used most often but black, silver, and copper are effective alternatives.

Peacock herl
Light and easy to apply, peacock herl possesses a natural iridescence that makes it ideal for a wide range of general nymph patterns.

Oval gold tinsel
Oval gold tinsel not only adds extra flash but also protects the delicate body material.

Lead wire
Where extra weight is required, the most effective ploy is to add close turns of lead wire before applying the body and thorax materials.

Brown cock hackles
Natural brown cock hackles add movement and give the impression of a nymph's legs. On patterns such as this, use a soft-fibered cock hackle or even a hen hackle to increase the action in the water.

3 At the same point as the goose biots, catch in 2 inches (5 cm) of fine oval gold tinsel. Next, catch in two strands of peacock herl by their tips.

4 Draw the strands of peacock herl forward so they are in line with the tying thread. Wind the herl over the thread for a couple of wraps before twisting them together to form a rope.

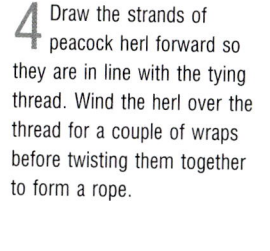

5 Wind the peacock herl and thread along the shank in close turns to form an even but chunky body. Continue winding the herl right up to the back of the bead.

6 Take the oval gold tinsel and wind it over the peacock herl in an opposite spiral. This method ensures that the tinsel crosses the turns of the herl and further locks them in place. That done, remove the excess.

7 Take a soft-fibered brown cock hackle. Prepare it and catch it in behind the bead, then wind on three turns. Take four strands of pearl Krystal Flash and catch them in halfway along their length.

8 Fold the strands over to create eight strands in all and secure them in place with thread turns. Cast off the tying thread with a whip finish before trimming the Krystal Flash to length.

See also   WEIGHTED UNDERBODY, PAGE 34

Wire Nymph

RECIPE

HOOK:	*Size 14–18 wet fly*
THREAD:	*Black*
BODY:	*Red wire*
HACKLE:	*Natural gray CDC*
THORAX:	*Black Ice Dub*

Colored wires are great for tying patterns such as this that need to be slim and able to cut quickly through the water's surface.

This is an up-to-date version of the extremely successful spider patterns that combined slim, wispy bodies and soft, highly mobile hackles to deadly effect. A range of soft hackles may be used, from hen hackles, waterhen, or starling to CDC in natural and dyed colors. The latter is particularly good, and its soft, mobile texture is finding its way into an increasing number of subsurface patterns. Various colored wires may be used for the body.

1 Place the hook securely in the vise and loop the wire over the shank a short distance from the bend.

FISH FOR:

Brown trout

Cutthroat

Rainbow trout

Grayling

2 Holding the wire so that it doesn't slip, begin winding it along the shank in close turns. Any gaps that do form may be closed by pushing the turns together.

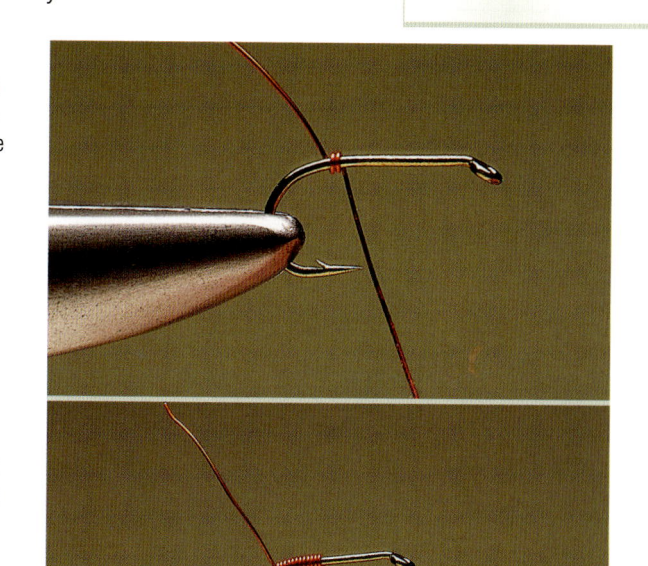

Black Ice Dub

The sparkle and fine texture of Ice Dub works well in many nymph patterns, either when used for the body or, as here, when used to form the thorax.

Red wire

For nymphs and spider patterns that need to be slim and quick to sink, wire makes an ideal body material. Various colors and combinations of colors may be used but red, black, and olive are still the most effective.

Natural CDC

CDC doesn't just work on dry flies; it also makes a superbly mobile hackle for subsurface patterns. It may be used either in its natural gray state or dyed in colors such as olive, tan, or even orange.

3 Continue winding the wire until it has covered three-quarters of the hook shank. Trim away the excess ends at both ends of the body.

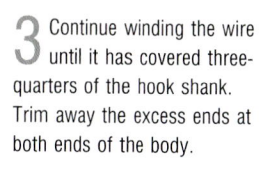

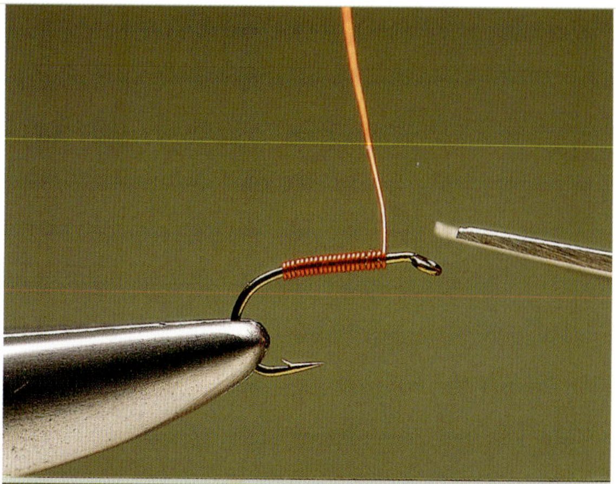

4 Run on a small drop of Superglue. Allow the glue to run in between all the turns. Leave the body to cure in a small block of foam.

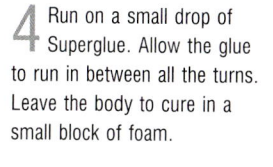

5 When the glue is no longer wet, run on tying thread just behind the eye. Dub on a very tiny pinch of black Ice Dub, waxing the thread first if necessary.

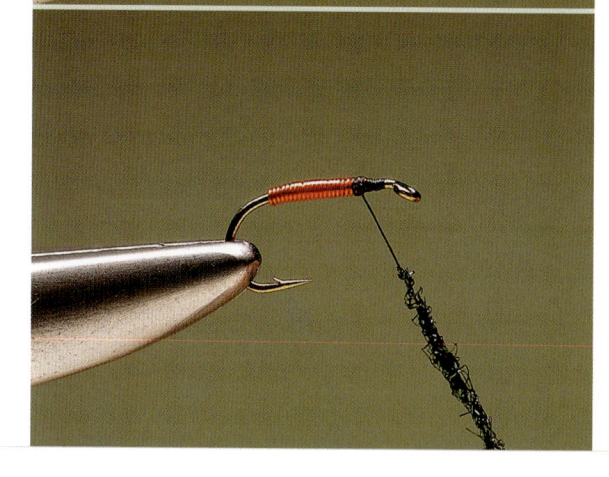

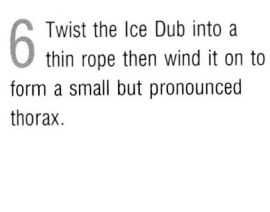

6 Twist the Ice Dub into a thin rope then wind it on to form a small but pronounced thorax.

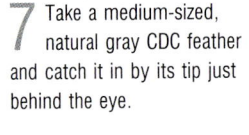

7 Take a medium-sized, natural gray CDC feather and catch it in by its tip just behind the eye.

8 Holding the feather by its base, wind on two or three turns, stroking the fibers back on each turn. Secure the loose end with thread and remove the excess. Cast off with a whip finish.

See also	DUBBING (SIMPLE), PAGE 28
	COLLAR HACKLE, PAGE 36

Shuttlecock

Though this fly might look a little strange with its large CDC wing, it is a superb imitation of a midge hatching at the surface. It is even taken by selective fish, which disregard the large wing and target the small slim body hanging beneath the surface.

When tying, don't skimp on the amount of CDC. Even on size 16 or 18 hooks at least three decent-sized plumes are required to keep it floating in the surface film. Also, choose feathers that are very soft and downy. If necessary remove the central stem from the plumes to prevent the wing from becoming overly stiff. Tied fat in olive, it makes a great floating snail imitation too.

RECIPE

HOOK:	*Size 14–18 mediumweight wet fly*
THREAD:	*Black*
RIB:	*Pearl Krystal Flash*
BODY:	*Peacock Ice Dub*
WING:	*Natural gray CDC*
THORAX:	*Orange dubbing*

1 Fix the hook in the vise and run the tying thread on at the eye. Carry it down the shank for a short distance, creating a solid base for the wing. Select a gray CDC feather with plenty of webby fibers.

FISH FOR:

Brown trout

Rainbow trout

2 Select another two or three feathers of identical size and place them together so that their tips are level. Catch them in so that the tips project over the eye of the hook.

Orange dubbing
When midges hatch at the surface for a few seconds there is an orange flush as blood is pumped through the wings. Here, orange fur is used to suggest this major trigger point.

Peacock Ice Dub
The fine lustrous material makes a perfect dubbing material where both sparkle and texture are required. It rags out well so all the fibers catch the light.

Natural gray CDC
The soft, naturally waterproofed plumes of CDC are the perfect material for all kinds of dry and emerger patterns. Here, multiple CDC plumes are used to create the shuttlecock that gives this pattern its name.

Pearl Krystal Flash
Krystal Flash is made up of fine strands of tinsel, each having a series of twists that allow the tiny facets that are created to sparkle at every turn. It is available in both metallic colors and various pearly ones such as olive lime and plain pearl.

3 Add further tight thread turns to secure the feathers firmly to the hook. Remove the waste ends of the feathers with scissors, angling them slightly to create a slight taper.

4 Carry the tying thread down to the bend in close turns, covering the ends of the CDC feathers. At a point opposite the barb catch in two strands of pearl Krystal Flash before dubbing on a small pinch of peacock Ice Dub.

5 Having created a slim, dubbed rope with the Ice Dub, wind it along the shank to produce a slim body. Stop where the bulge of the CDC waste ends begins.

6 Take hold of the strands of Krystal Flash and twist them gently together. Wind them, without stretching, over the body in five open, evenly spaced turns.

7 Once the end of the body has been reached, secure the ends of the Krystal Flash and remove the excess. Dub on a small pinch of orange fur and wind on to form a small, pronounced thorax.

8 Carry the thread forward to the eye and apply a few turns to lift the wing slightly. Finally, cast off the tying thread with a whip finish. Apply a drop of lacquer to the head, taking care that it doesn't wick into the CDC.

See also   RIBBING SET, PAGE 22

DUBBING (SIMPLE), PAGE 28

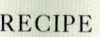

Pink Shrimp

This is a superb pattern for both trout and grayling, especially when trundled slowly along the riverbed. The bright color works even when the water is clear and the fish selective. Though this pattern is not tied to be imitative, the profile is just like that of a real shrimp or scud. So by substituting olive or gray materials for the pink, the pattern can easily be tied as a direct imitation.

To help the fly sink, turns of lead wire are applied to the hook before the rest of the materials. A thin plastic strip stretched over the back of the fly and combined with teased out dubbing, gives it a very lifelike appearance.

RECIPE

HOOK:	*Size 14–16 heavyweight grub or shrimp hook*
THREAD:	*Fluorescent pink*
WEIGHT:	*Lead wire*
RIB:	*Fine, clear nylon monofilament*
SHELL BACK:	*Translucent pink plastic strip*
BODY:	*Pink dubbing fur*

1 Fix the hook in the vise and form an underbody from turns of lead wire. Secure the wire with close wraps of tying thread before catching in 3 inches (7.5 cm) of clear nylon monofilament at the hook bend.

FISH FOR:

Brown trout

Grayling

Rainbow trout

2 Take a translucent pink plastic strip and catch it in at the bend, shiny side up. Allow the waste end of the plastic strip to fold around the body before securing it and the waste ends of the monofilament with thread.

Pink dubbing

Pink dubbing is used to form the body of this pattern though olive or tan may also be used to produce a more lifelike effect. If using a manmade dubbing choose one such as SLF, which is quite coarse and teases out to suggest the creature's legs.

Nylon monofilament

Various ribbing materials may be used to lock a shell back to the body. Here it is clear, nylon monofilament that is tough, invisible and produces a nice segmented effect.

Lead wire

Winding close turns of lead wire on the hook before adding the rest of the materials produces a quick sinking pattern ideal for fishing in deep or fast flowing water.

Plastic strip

Thin flexible plastic strip is an ideal material for producing the shell back on patterns such as caddis pupae and scuds or shrimps. It comes in a range of natural colors plus more colorful ones including yellow, red, and pink.

3 Take a large pinch of pink dubbing fur and apply it to the waxed tying thread. Dub it onto the thread to form a thick rope. Starting where the plastic strip was tied in, wind the dubbing in close turns over the underbody.

4 Continue winding the dubbed fur in close turns, making sure that no gaps form. As there is no wing or hackle to be added, the fur body should be wound almost up to the eye.

5 Next, draw the plastic strip over the back of the body, allowing it to mold itself around the sides. Stretch the strip a little before securing it at the eye with a couple of thread wraps.

6 Take hold of the nylon monofilament and wind it over the back and body. This has the effect of securing the plastic strip in place. Apply the rib in open, evenly spaced turns.

7 When the rib has almost reached the eye, unwind the two thread turns, holding the plastic strip there. Do not let go of the monofilament at this point but secure it with tight thread turns.

8 Now, simply fold the plastic strip back to the eye and secure it with thread turns. Remove the excess strip and monofilament before casting off with a whip finish. Finally, tease out the fibers under the hook to suggest legs.

See also   DUBBING (SIMPLE), PAGE 28

WEIGHTED UNDERBODY, PAGE 34

Hydropsyche

RECIPE

HOOK: *Size 10–16 Grub Hook*

THREAD: *White*

WEIGHT: *Lead wire*

TAIL: *Gray partridge down*

RIB: *Fine, clear nylon monofilament*

BACK: *Tan plastic strip*

BODY: *Cream fur*

THORAX: *Hare's fur*

Hydropsyche are caddis flies with free-swimming larvae that don't build cases until it is time to pupate. For this reason they are heavily predated upon by both trout and grayling. As a coincidence, the Hydropsyche's body shape makes it ideal for packing in plenty of weight. The result is a fly that gets right to the killing zone close to the riverbed while still looking very natural.

White thread works perfectly when applying cream fur but brown thread should be used for dubbing the darker thorax. Instead of changing the thread the white thread may simply be colored with a brown marker pen.

1 Apply a weighted underbody formed from lead wire wound well around the bend. Secure the lead wire in place with tying thread before catching in a small pinch of gray partridge down at the rear of the underbody.

FISH FOR:

Brown trout

2 At the same point as the partridge feather, catch in 3 inches (7.5 cm) of clear nylon monofilament plus a strip of tan plastic, shiny side up. The plastic strip is molded around the sides of the underbody.

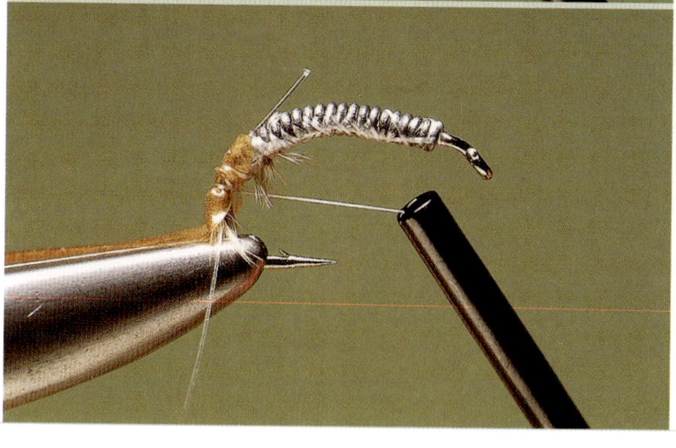

Grayling

Rainbow trout

Lead wire
Lead wire works extremely well for adding weight to patterns such as the Hydropsyche. Close turns in either a single or double layer are applied before any other materials are added and sit concealed beneath the body and thorax.

Nylon monofilament
When a lifelike segmentation is required clear nylon monofilament is useful because it doesn't affect the overall color of the fly but does bite into the body and give it definition. It also keeps the plastic shellback firmly in place.

Tan plastic strip
This thin, flexible plastic strip is both translucent and stretchy so it fits snugly around the top and sides of the body. It is available in a range of colors, with natural hues such as olive, brown, and tan the most effective.

Brown partridge down
This is normally a waste material but makes a nice mobile tail and imitates the little pseudo legs at the tip of the larva's abdomen.

Cream fur
This should be fine textured and preferably manmade so that it doesn't absorb too much water. SLF Finesse is a very good product but there are similar products available under different brands.

Hare's fur
The mottled browns of hare's fur are used here to suggest the darker thorax area.

3 Wax the thread, then dub on a pinch of cream fur. Using a simple finger-and-thumb twist, form a thin yarn, then wind it in close turns so that it covers three-quarters of the underbody.

4 As the next material to be applied has a brown hue, the thread may either be changed or colored with a marker pen so that it matches the hare's fur more closely.

5 Dub on a good pinch of hare's fur, first ensuring that there are plenty of the stiffer guard hairs in the mix to produce a nice "buggy" feel.

6 Once the fur has reached the eye stretch the plastic strip over the back of both body and thorax before securing it just behind the eye with a couple of thread turns.

7 Wind the nylon monofilament toward the eye in evenly spaced turns, locking the plastic strip in place. Once the monofilament has reached the eye, release the plastic strip and secure the loose end of the monofilament with thread.

8 Remove the excess monofilament, then refix the plastic strip. Add further thread turns, then remove the excess plastic strip. Build a small head and cast off with a whip finish. Finally, color the top of the thorax with a brown marker pen.

See also   RIBBING SET, PAGE 22

WEIGHTED UNDERBODY, PAGE 34

CDC Sparkle Dun

RECIPE

HOOK: *Size 14–20 light wire dry fly*

THREAD: *Olive*

TAIL: *White or olive antron*

BODY: *Olive SLF Finesse*

WING: *Natural gray CDC plus a few fibers of lemon wood duck*

THORAX: *Olive*

A standard mayfly pattern, the Sparkle Dun is a variant of the original Compara Dun, which used a semicircular wing of deer hair instead of a normal hackle to keep the fly floating. What made it a Sparkle Dun was the use of clear antron for the tail, the aim being to imitate the empty shuck of the nymph. This has proved to be an important recognition point and definitely improves the effectiveness of the pattern. A further enhancement is the use of CDC for the wing. This may be used on its own but on patterns tied to imitate mayflies with mottled wings, a pinch of lemon wood duck may be added.

1 Having fixed the hook in the vise, run the tying thread on at the eye. A short distance back from the eye catch in a few fibers of lemon wood duck, then select two large CDC feathers.

FISH FOR:

Brown trout

Cutthroat

Rainbow trout

2 Place the CDC feathers together so that their tips are perfectly level. Catch them in on top of the wood duck fibers so they project over the eye of the hook.

Natural CDC
There are few feathers more ideal for tying dry fly wings than CDC. Here, natural CDC both helps the fly to float as well as copying the color of a small mayfly's wings.

Olive antron yarn
Olive or clear antron gives a wonderful sparkle as well as imitating the shuck of the hatching insect.

Lemon wood duck
Lemon wood duck or dyed gray mallard flank may be used to add a mottled effect to imitations of certain mayfly species. If the one you are copying has plain gray wings, simply leave it out.

Olive dubbing
This finely textured man-made dubbing comes in a wide range of brands and colors, making them perfect for tying small dry flies.

3 Using sharp scissors, trim away the waste ends of the CDC at an angle so they create a taper. This will help to give the finished body a natural profile.

4 Cover the waste ends of the CDC with close thread turns. When the thread has reached a point opposite the hook barb, catch in a few fibers of clear or olive antron.

5 Take a pinch of fine olive dubbing and apply it evenly to the thread. Create a slim rope using either a dubbing loop or a simple finger-and-thumb twist.

6 Starting at the base of the tail, wind the dubbed fur along the shank in close turns. Make sure that there are no gaps and that a gradual taper is formed.

7 When the body has reached right to the base of the wing, wind the bare thread up to the eye. Push the wing into an upright position. This will cause the fibers to flare around the top and sides of the body.

8 Apply another pinch of the fine olive dubbing and wind this tight up against the front of the wing to hold it in place. Carry the dubbing on up to the eye and cast off with a whip finish. Finally, trim the tail to length.

See also   DUBBING (SIMPLE), PAGE 28

Flexi Buzzer

RECIPE

HOOK:	*Size 8–14 heavyweight grub hook*
THREAD:	*Black*
BODY:	*Black and white strands of Flexi Floss*
WING CASE:	*Fluorescent orange floss*
THORAX:	*Black tying thread*
THORAX COVER:*	*Wide, flat pearl tinsel*

The Flexi Buzzer is designed to imitate the pupa of a Chironomid midge and can be tied in a wide range of colors to imitate the various species that are found in both lakes and rivers. The stretchy Lycra-based product used for its body is marketed under brand names such as Flexi Floss, Super Floss, and Spanflex. It is a superb material, not only for tying the bodies of nymphs but for use as a ribbing material. In can also be used in place of the standard rubber legs where action needs to be imparted to the fly.

In addition to using a single color of Flexi Floss, various colors can be put together to produce a range of interesting effects.

1 Fix the hook in the vise and having run on the tying thread a short distance from the eye, catch in the two strands of Flexi Floss with tight thread wraps. Stretch the floss to reduce its bulk using close turns of thread to fix it to the hook.

FISH FOR:

Brown trout

Rainbow trout

2 Continue until the thread and floss have been carried well around the bend to give the finished body a curved profile. Run the thread back up toward the eye, then stretch the floss and wind it in close turns.

Flexi Floss—black and white

This Lycra-based material is sold under a range of brand names such as Stretch Floss, Super Floss, and Spanflex. Being super-stretchy it is ideal for creating slim bodies on nymphs and pupae or for ribbing. It may be used either in single colors or in a combination to suggest the mottled colors of some insects or to mimic their segmentation.

Pearl tinsel

As they are about to transform from pupa to adult many aquatic insects exhibit a noticeable sparkle caused by gasses trapped under their skin. The addition of pearl tinsel either along the body or as a thorax cover gives just the right amount of flash.

Orange fluorescent floss

Chironomid or buzzer pupae have pronounced orange wing buds that form a major trigger point. These can be imitated using a variety of materials including fluorescent floss where the highly visible color makes the pattern even more effective.

3 When winding two colors of floss together make sure they do not twist; this will keep the colors separate and in the same order after each turn. With the body complete, secure the ends of the floss and remove the excess.

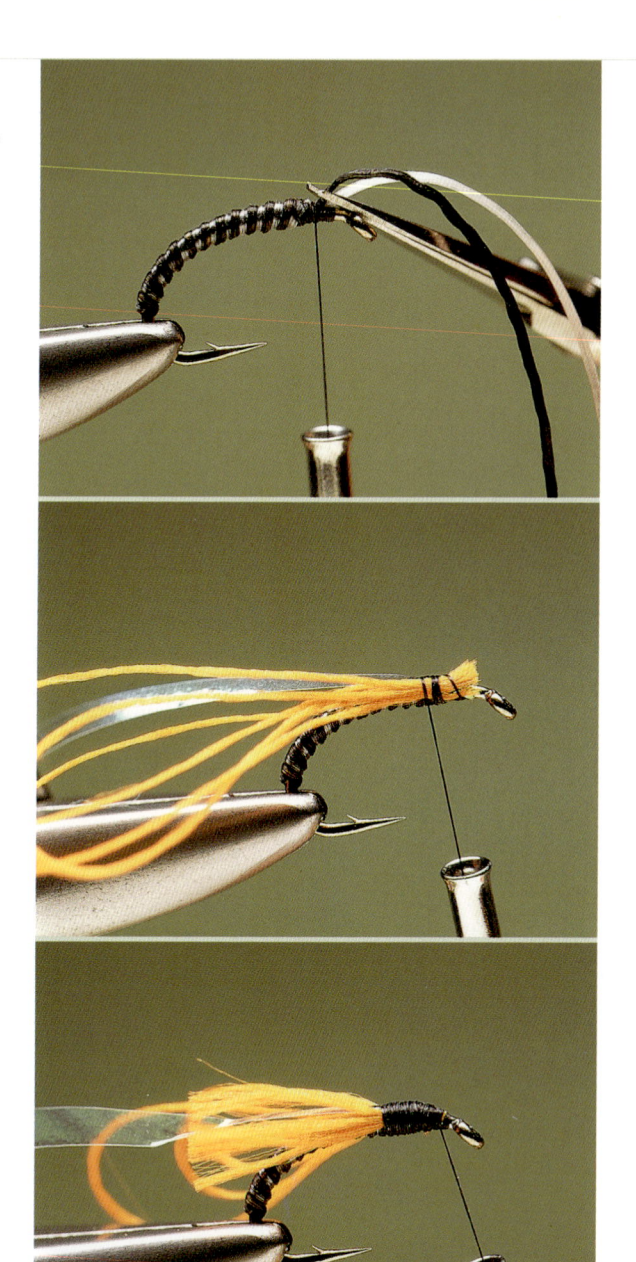

4 Secure an inch (2.5 cm) or so of pearl tinsel at the front of the body. Take a strand of fluorescent orange floss and fold it twice to form four strands. Catch them in on the near side of the body.

5 Repeat the process on the far side of the body. An easy method is simply to cut off the extra floss already applied and add it to the far side. Create a pronounced thorax with close turns of tying thread.

6 With the tying thread positioned at the eye, draw the ends of the floss strands forward to create an orange cheek running on either side of the thorax. Secure the ends of the floss with tight thread turns.

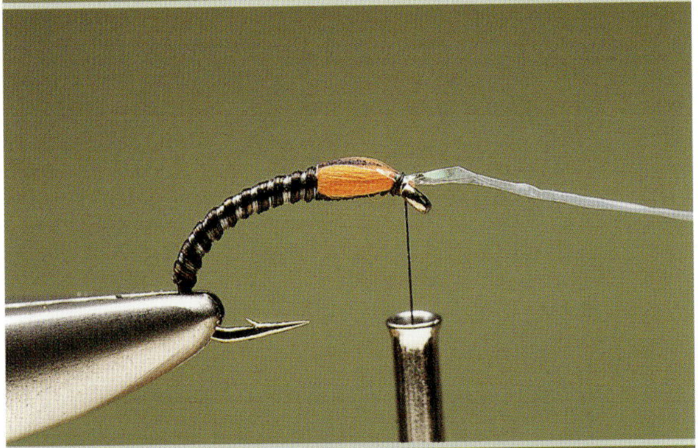

7 Carefully remove the excess floss using scissors, then draw the flat pearl tinsel over the top of the thorax and secure it with tying thread. Do not stretch the tinsel but simply pull so that it sits tight on the thorax top.

8 Remove the excess tinsel and build a small, neat head. Cast off the tying thread with a whip finish, then apply one or two coats of clear lacquer to the entire fly. This will give a smooth finish and make the fly extremely robust.

See also   RIBBING SET, PAGE 22

Hatching Midge

This is a brilliant little pattern—deadly either on a river or lake. Midges make up a large part of the trout's diet and are often targeted as the adults hatch in the surface film. Trout can be picky when it comes to taking these emerging flies and it is important to get the profile of any imitation absolutely right. This pattern uses a combination of CDC plus a couple of turns of grizzly cock hackle to float the fly just like the real thing. The addition of the antron tail imitates the clear shuck of the pupa left behind after the adult emerges. A few turns of pearl Krystal Flash mimic the sparkle created by gases trapped under the midge's skin.

RECIPE

HOOK:	*Size 14–20 mediumweight hook*
THREAD:	*Black*
TAIL:	*White antron*
RIB:	*Pearl Krystal Flash*
BODY:	*Dyed black rabbit fur*
HACKLE:	*Grizzly cock hackle*
THORAX:	*Peacock herl*
THORAX COVER:	*Natural gray CDC*

1 Having fixed the hook in the vise, run the tying thread down the shank in close turns. At a point opposite the barb catch in a slim length of white antron plus 2-inch (5-cm) pearl Krystal Flash.

FISH FOR:

Brown trout

Cutthroat

Rainbow trout

2 Cover the waste ends of the antron and Krystal Flash with close turns of thread. This builds up an even base for the body. Dub on a small pinch of dyed black rabbit or muskrat fur and wind along the shank.

Pearl Krystal Flash
This adds a nice sparkle that mimics that produced by gases trapped in the natural's body.

Peacock herl
Peacock herl is light and easy to work with, and possesses a natural iridescence.

Natural CDC
The softness and natural buoyancy of CDC make it ideal for using in patterns intended to float right in the surface film. Gray works fine but try orange here instead to mimic the flush of color found in a hatching midge.

White antron
The sparkle and translucency of this material make it great for imitating the shuck of an emerging aquatic insect such as the midge.

Black rabbit fur
This natural material dubs easily and works well for either the body or thorax on a whole range of dark nymph patterns. Allowing a few of the stiffer guard hairs to stick out increases the bug effect.

Grizzly cock hackles
The gray and white speckling of grizzly hackles are great for imitating the general buzz of an insect's legs and wings.

3 Continue winding the dubbed fur in close turns until it has covered two-thirds of the hook shank, thus forming the body. Next, take hold of the Krystal Flash and wind it over the body in four or five evenly spaced turns.

4 Secure the loose end of the Krystal Flash and remove the excess. That done, take two gray CDC plumes, place them together, tips level, and catch them in so they project just past the tail.

5 Take a short-fibered grizzly cock hackle. Prepare it in the normal way and catch it in at the base of the CDC plumes. At the same point, catch in a single strand of peacock herl.

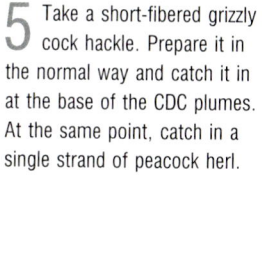

6 Wind the tying thread up to the eye. Take hold of the peacock herl and, without twisting, wind it in close turns up to the eye. Secure the loose end with thread turns.

7 Take hold of the hackletip with hackle pliers and wind on two or three open, evenly spaced turns. Secure the hackletip with thread and remove the excess.

8 Draw the CDC plumes over the back of the thorax, if necessary trimming away the hackle fibers on top of the thorax first. Secure the CDC at the eye, leaving the tips projecting over it. Cast off with a whip finish.

See also   RIBBING SET, PAGE 22

DUBBING (SIMPLE), PAGE 28

Sparklewinged Spinner

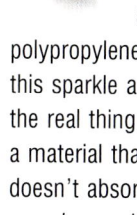

RECIPE

HOOK:	*Size 14–22*
THREAD:	*Brown or white*
TAIL:	*Blue dun*
BODY:	*Rusty brown dubbing—SLF Finesse*
WING:	*White polypropylene yarn and pearl Lite Brite*
THORAX:	*Rusty brown dubbing—SLF Finesse*

The first thing you notice when watching spent spinners drifting downstream are those clear, sparkling wings trapped in the surface film. The Sparklewinged Spinner uses a blend of white polypropylene yarn with a touch of pearl Lite Brite to mimic this sparkle as well as to form wings that sit outstretched like the real thing. When tying spinner wings, it is important to use a material that floats either naturally, such as CDC, or one that doesn't absorb water and is easily treated with a floatant such as polypropylene yarn. The tails are splayed out to support the rear end of the fly.

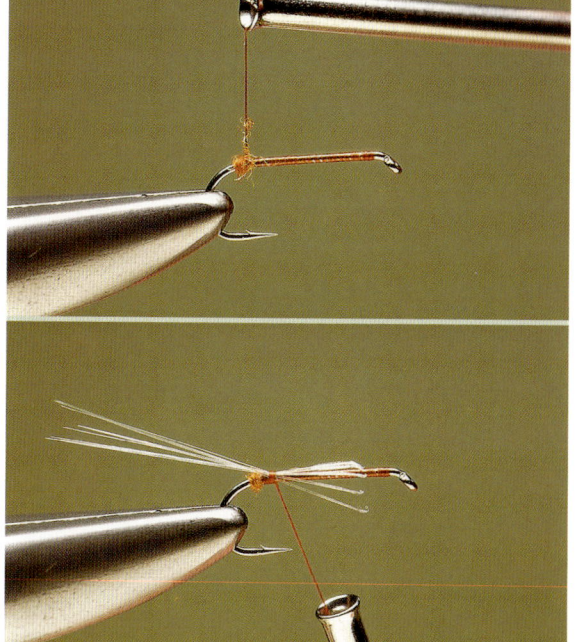

1 With the hook secured in the vise, run tying thread down the shank to a point opposite the barb. Dub on a minute pinch of the same fur used for the body and create a small ball.

FISH FOR:

Brown trout

Cutthroat

Rainbow trout

2 Remove a few fibers from a large blue dun cock hackle. Making sure that they are straight, catch them in so that they project past the bend and sit on top of the tiny dubbing ball.

Rusty brown dubbing—SLF Finesse
Rusty brown dubbing is perfect for the body of patterns imitating small Baetis spinners. The color should be changed to match that of the species being imitated.

Blue dun cock hackle fibers
The large hackles that run down the sides of the cape have long, straight fibers ideal for using as tails on dry flies.

Pearl Lite Brite
Lite Brite is a fine iridescent material that comes in a range of colors and adds a sparkle to any fly. Here, the green pearl version is used to give a natural-looking sparkle to the spinner's wings.

White polypropylene yarn
This man-made yarn is very light and has a stiffness that makes it ideal for spinner wings. It floats exceptionally well, especially if treated with a good floatant.

3 Cover the waste ends of the hackle fibers with close turns of tying thread. Next, apply a pinch of the body material to the thread using a dubbing loop to create a fine, tightly spun rope.

4 Begin to wind the dubbed fur along the shank. The first turn should be made tight up against the ball of dubbing fur. This turn will force the hackle fibers down and cause them to splay out.

5 Continue winding the fur along the shank in close turns to create a slim, slightly tapered body. When three-quarters of the hook shank has been covered, secure the loose ends with thread.

6 Remove the waste end of the dubbing, then take a short length of white polypropylene yarn plus a few strands of pearl Lite Brite. Catch them in halfway along their length on top of the hook.

7 Twist the polypropylene yarn and Lite Brite so that they sit at 90 degrees to the hook shank to create the spent-wing profile. Fix the wing in place with figure-of-eight turns of thread.

8 With the wings in place, dub on another small pinch of dubbing, winding it around the wing roots to form a thorax. Finally, cast off the thread with a whip finish and trim the wings to length.

See also   SPINNER WING, PAGE 20

DUBBING (SIMPLE), PAGE 28

Soldier Palmer

The Soldier Palmer, as its name suggests, has a hackle running the length of its body. This technique is known as "palmering." It is one used for most fly types, either where the extra hackle turns can help the fly to float, as in the case of dry flies, or for streamers and wet flies, as here, where it gives movement to the pattern.

This is a traditional lake pattern, designed for use as part of a three-fly team. Its dense water-moving profile, provided by the two hackles, make it a great fly for dibbling through the wave tops. Though having a long pedigree, here it has been given a modern twist by the addition of a tail of fluorescent red floss.

1 Having run on a layer of tying thread, take a length of fluorescent red floss, fold it three times to make it eight times as thick, and catch it in at the bend. At the same point catch in 3 inches (7.5 cm) of fine, oval gold tinsel.

2 Cover the waste ends of the floss and the tinsel with close turns of thread. This fixes them to the hook and creates an even base for the body. Remove any excess material, thus trimming the tail to length.

Oval gold tinsel
Fine, oval gold tinsel is used here both to impart some sparkle into the body and also to lock the turns of the body hackle securely in place.

Red dubbing
Traditionally this pattern called for dyed seal's fur but modern substitutes such as SLF are equally good. These can be ragged out after applying to impart translucency into an otherwise solid outline.

Fluorescent floss
A hot spot of a fluorescent material adds a kick to any fly. Here red fluorescent floss is used to give this traditional wet fly a modern twist. Short sections of this floss may also be added to the red fur used for the body.

Brown cock hackle
For palmered wet flies a hackle with fibers of medium stiffness is required; not dry-fly quality but something that will still impart some movement into the finished fly.

3 Apply a light coating of wax to the tying thread, then, using a simple finger-and-thumb twist, dub on a pinch of red seal's fur. Wind the resulting rope in close turns so that it covers the hook, leaving a small gap at the eye.

4 Select a soft brown cock hackle with a fiber length around one-and-a-half times that of the hook gape. Strip the fibers from its base and catch it in at the very front of the body.

5 Remove the excess hackle stem before taking hold of the hackletip with a pair of hackle pliers. Wind the hackle down toward the tail in open, evenly spaced turns. Keep light tension on the hackle at all times.

6 Once the hackle has reached the tail, take the gold tinsel and begin to wind it up through the hackle. Take care when winding the rib that it only locks the stem of the hackle into place and doesn't trap any fibers.

7 Once the rib has reached the eye, secure the loose end with tight turns of the tying thread. Only now can the tension be relieved and the excess tip removed carefully using scissors.

8 Trim away the excess tinsel at the eye before catching in a second brown hackle with a fiber length a little greater than the first. Wind on three turns to form a collar. Secure and remove the tip before casting off with a whip finish.

| See also | RIBBING SET, PAGE 22 |
| | COLLAR HACKLE, PAGE 36 |

Pale Morning Dun

PMD, short for Pale Morning Dun, is the name used for a range of very small, pale-colored mayfly duns. Because of the small size of the fly it is important to use an ultrafine dubbing such as SLF Finesse or similar. Thread diameter too needs to be as low as possible with 6/0 a basic requirement and 8/0 the ideal. Fine thread helps prevent excessive bulk from forming, which ruins what should be a very delicate-looking fly.

The use of the thorax-tie hackle means that the turns are evenly distributed along the thorax rather than applied as a collar. The result is a more natural footprint on the water's surface.

RECIPE

HOOK:	*Size 14–20 light-wire dry fly*
THREAD:	*Yellow*
TAIL:	*Honey dun cock hackle fibers*
BODY:	*Cream fur*
WING:	*Dyed gray turkey flats*
HACKLE:	*Honey or light blue dun cock hackle*
THORAX:	*Cream fur*

1 Fix the hook in the vise and run on a bed of tying thread just behind the eye. Remove a section of gray turkey flat double the width of the intended wing.

FISH FOR:

Brown trout

Cutthroat

Rainbow trout

2 Fold the strip of turkey flat in half, then catch it in one-third of the shank's length back from the eye. Make sure that the tips of the feather project over the eye.

Turkey flats
Alternatively known as coquille these are turkey body feathers that have a flat appearance and a soft, webby texture. They are easy to work with and produce an easy-to-tie wing on a wide range of small mayfly imitations.

Cream fur
This should be fine textured and preferably man-made so that it doesn't absorb too much water. SLF Finesse is a very good product but there are similar products under different brands.

Honey dun cock hackles
These are light honey-colored hackles that are the perfect color for both the hackle and tail of tiny, pale-colored mayflies such as the Pale Morning Dun and the Pale Watery.

3 Trim the waste ends of the turkey flat to create a slight taper, then use turns of tying thread to secure it to the hook. Dub on a tiny pinch of cream fur, applying it as a small ball at the hook bend.

4 Take a few fibers of honey-colored cock hackle and catch them in just in front of the dubbed ball. Secure them with tight thread turns.

5 Dub on a second, larger pinch of cream fur. Use a simple finger-and-thumb twist to create a fine, tapered rope. Make the first turn of the dubbing tight against the ball to splay the tail fibers, then carry on toward the wing.

6 Having created a fine, tapered body, stop just behind the wing. Select a cock hackle with fiber length approximately one-and-a-half times that of the hook gape. Prepare and catch it in just behind the wing.

7 Take a third pinch of the cream fur and dub that too onto the tying thread. Wind one turn behind the wing, then the rest from the front of the wing to the eye. This forms the thorax.

8 Using hackle pliers, take hold of the hackle by its tip and wind two open turns behind the wing. Wind another three open, evenly spaced turns in front of the wing. Secure the excess at the eye and remove.

See also   DUBBING (SIMPLE), PAGE 28

Blue-winged Olive

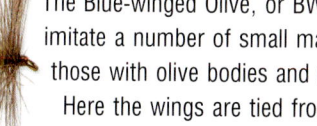

The Blue-winged Olive, or BWO, is a pattern tied to imitate a number of small mayfly species, typically those with olive bodies and smoky gray wings.
Here the wings are tied from hackle points positioned upright to mimic the profile of the real mayfly. This technique produces a delicate effect in keeping with an imitation of such a small fly.

The main problem with tying hackle-point wings is fixing them securely so they don't pull out when the fly is cast. The best way is simply to leave the stripped stems long and fix the hackles with thread, having first drawn them back between the two hackles.

HOOK:	*Size 14–22 light wire dry fly*
THREAD:	*Olive*
TAIL:	*Blue dun cock hackle fibers*
BODY:	*Olive SLF Finesse*
WING:	*Blue dun cock hackletips*
HACKLE:	*Blue dun cock hackle*

1 Secure the hook in the vise and run on the tying thread a short distance from the eye. Strip two matching blue dun cock hackles to leave two tips and catch them in with two thread turns.

FISH FOR:

Brown trout

Cutthroat

Rainbow trout

Grayling

2 Lift the tips into an upright position and secure with thread turns. Part the tips before drawing stripped hackle stems between them. Secure the stems with thread, to fix the wings firmly.

Blue dun cock hackles
These hackles are not blue at all but various shades of gray. They are available as dyed or natural, the latter being considerably more expensive but offering more subtle shades and markings. Like other hackle colors they come either as neck or saddle hackles.

Olive SLF Finesse
Olive Finesse has just the right color and texture for producing the body on a wide range of small, olive-bodied mayflies. Being very fine it helps to produce the slim body required in such small, imitative patterns.

3 Take the thread in close turns down to the hook bend. Opposite the barb catch in a few fibers of blue dun cock hackle to form the tail. That done, wax the thread lightly and apply a small pinch of fine olive fur.

4 Twist the fur and thread together to form a fine, dubbed rope that has a slight taper. Beginning at the tail base, wind the dubbed fur along the shank in close turns. Stop when the fur has reached the wings.

5 Select a blue dun cock hackle with a fiber length approximately one-and-a-half times that of the hook gape. Hackle size may be measured by looping the hackle over the hook shank so that it flares.

6 Once the correct-sized hackle has been chosen, prepare it by stripping away any damaged fibers from the base. Using tying thread, catch the hackle in at the wing base by a short stub of bare stem.

7 Take hold of the hackle by its tip, using a pair of hackle pliers. Wind two close turns of hackle behind the wings.

8 Wind a further three turns of hackle in front of the wings before securing the loose end of the hackle at the eye with tying thread. Trim off the excess hackletip with scissors. Finally, cast off the thread with a whip finish.

See also   DUBBING (SIMPLE), PAGE 28

HACKLETIP WING, PAGE 32

CDC Greendrake

The CDC (cul-de-canard) Greendrake is a very effective imitation of the dun stage of various species of large, pale mayflies. To the entomologist this immature, winged stage of the mayfly is known as the sub imago, but to the angler it is the dun or Greendrake.

The pattern is tied with a wing of cul-de-canard feathers, which are located close to a duck's preen gland. These feathers not only have a soft, downy texture but are impregnated with the natural oil the duck uses to waterproof its plumage. The result is a feather that is both translucent and floats well—ideal, in fact, for the wings of all kinds of dry mayfly patterns.

RECIPE

HOOK:	*Size 8–10 mediumweight longshank*
THREAD:	*Yellow*
TAIL:	*Fibers of moose mane*
RIB:	*Thick, brown tying thread*
BODY:	*Cream fur*
WING:	*Natural CDC*
HACKLE:	*Grizzly cock hackle*
THORAX:	*Cream fur*

1 Fix the hook in the vise and run the tying thread down the shank in close turns. Select four or five fibers of moose mane. Ensure that none are damaged before catching them in at the hook bend to form the tail.

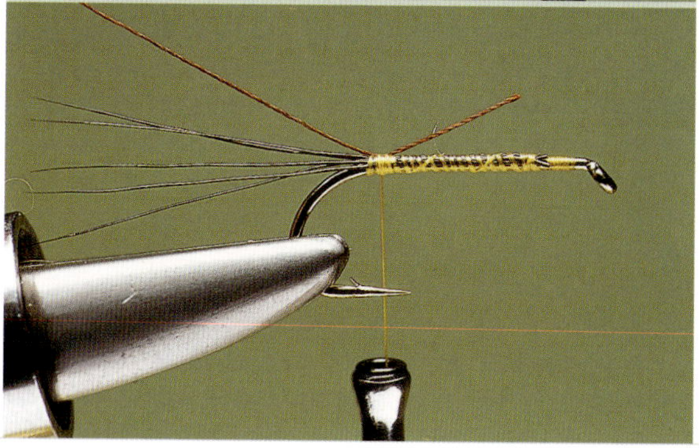

FISH FOR:

Brown trout

Cutthroat

Rainbow trout

2 Secure the moose-mane fibers with tight thread turns, locking the waste ends to the shank to form an even base for the body. At the tail base, catch in 3 inches (7.5cm) of brown thread.

Natural CDC

Straight from the duck, cul-de-canard comes in various shades of gray. The soft, downy plumes make great wings for a wide variety of insect imitations such as the Greendrake.

Moose mane

The stiff fibers of moose mane work well as a tail material on a number of large dry flies.

Grizzly cock hackles

The gray and white speckling of grizzly hackles makes an effective impression of legs and wings on many top dry-fly patterns.

Brown thread

Thick brown tying thread of around 6/0 denier makes a perfect ribbing material for large dry flies, where the extra weight of metal wire is inappropriate for a fly designed to float.

Cream fur

The body of this fly is formed from dubbed cream fur. This can be any manmade fur such as SLF or a polypropylene or antron-based material.

3 Take a large pinch of cream fur. Apply it evenly to the tying thread, which should be lightly waxed. Dub the fur onto the thread to form a tapered rope and wind it from the tail base along the hook shank.

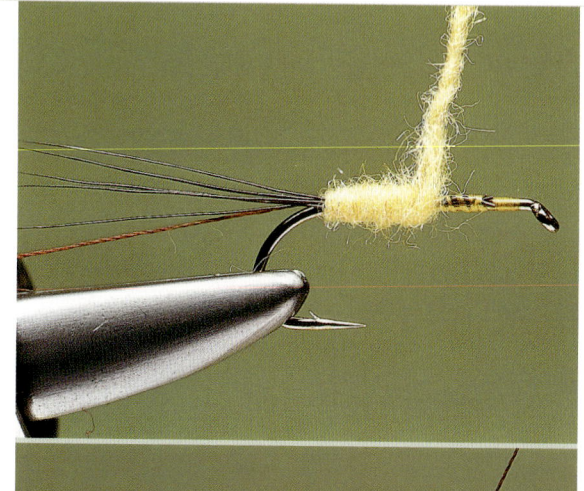

4 Stop the body when three-quarters of the shank has been covered. Wind the brown thread over the fur body in open, evenly spaced turns. Adding two sets of close turns near to the tail mimics the markings of the natural fly.

5 Secure the loose end of the ribbing material with tying thread then select two large CDC feathers. These should be exactly the same size with plenty of downy fibers. Place them together so their tips are level, and position the feathers, with thread, in front of the body.

6 With the tip of the wing projecting just past the hook bend, fix the CDC feathers in place with tight thread turns. Remove the waste ends with scissors then select a grizzle cock hackle with fiber length one-and-a-half times the hook gape. Catch the hackle in by its base, just in front of the body.

7 Secure the hackle in place by winding tight thread turns over a short section of bare hackle stem. Dub on a small pinch of the same cream-colored fur as used for the body. Wind it on behind the wing then up to the eye to form the thorax.

8 Use hackle pliers to grip the tip of the cock hackle. Wind on two open turns behind the wing then carry the hackle on in front of the wing. Wind on a further two or three open turns of hackle before securing the hackletip at the eye. Remove the excess then cast off the thread with a whip finish.

See also   RIBBING SET, PAGE 22

DUBBING (SIMPLE), PAGE 28

Mayfly Cripple

This is a simple little pattern designed to imitate an emerging or stillborn mayfly dun. Selective trout will often pick off these cripples in preference to the more agile, viable duns.

This is the pheasant tail version that mimics the darker mayfly species. Depending on the hatch, it can be tied in olive or cream with equal success. In all versions of this pattern the profile is the same. The forward-pointing deer hair wing creates a lifelike effect and adds buoyancy.

When tying feather fiber bodies, especially on dry flies or emergers, a rib of nylon monofilament works better than wire.

HOOK:	*Size 14–20 dry fly*
THREAD:	*Brown*
TAIL:	*Cock pheasant tail fibers*
RIB:	*Clear nylon monofilament (optional)*
BODY:	*Cock pheasant tail fibers*
WING:	*Natural deer hair*
HACKLE:	*Dark gray cock hackle*
THORAX:	*Hare's fur*

1 With the hook secured firmly in the vise, run the thread down to the bend in close turns. There catch in three pheasant tail fibers so the tips form the tails.

FISH FOR:

Brown trout

Cutthroat

Rainbow trout

2 Catch in three or more pheasant tail fibers by their tips and carry the thread up the shank in close turns. Apply a light coat of flexible adhesive cement, which will protect the delicate fibers.

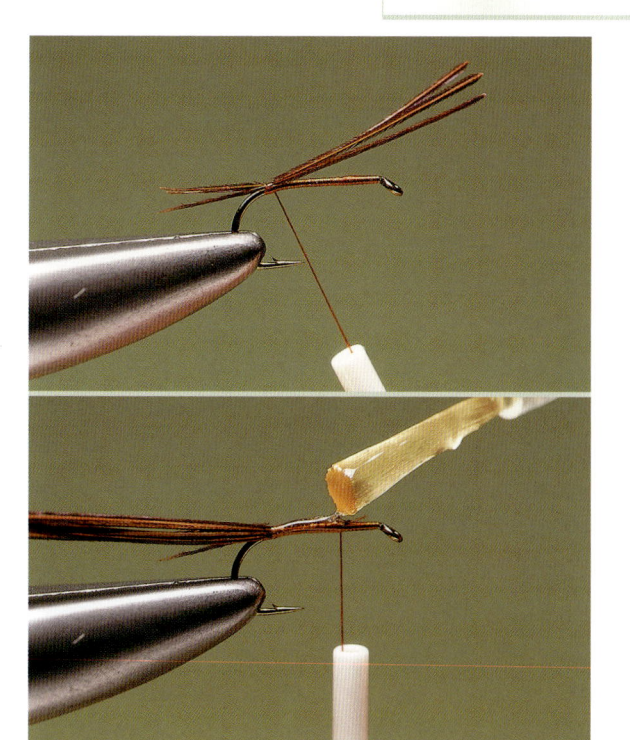

Hare's fur

A pinch of pale hare's fur is used here to mimic the light flush around the thorax area of a hatching mayfly. Keeping a few of the stiffer guard hairs in the mix helps suggest the general buzz of legs and wings.

Clear nylon monofilament

Where a rib is needed, such as on a pattern like a tiny dry fly or emerger, the added weight of wire is not appropriate. A great alternative is to use a fine, clear monofilament nylon that protects the body materials and adds negligible weight.

Natural deer hair

A few fibers of natural deer hair tied with the tips projecting over the hook eye suggest the wing of an emerging mayfly or that of a crippled insect unable to take flight. The hollow butts also add a small amount of buoyancy and help the fly to float.

Dark gray cock hackles

Cock hackles are available in a wide range of colors and shades. Gray, or Blue Dun as it is often known, is a prime example being a great feather to use when imitating the gray wings of a small mayfly.

Cock pheasant tail fibers

The tail fibers of the male ring-necked pheasant make a superb body material for tying all types of nymphs and dry flies. Here it is used to suggest the body of a small, dark mayfly.

3 Once the cement has dried to a tacky consistency (this only takes a few seconds), wind the pheasant tail fibers in close turns, allowing them to spread flat so that a slim, slightly tapered body is formed.

4 When the pheasant tail fibers have covered two-thirds of the hook shank, secure the loose ends with two or three tight thread turns and trim away the excess with scissors.

5 Apply a little wax to the thread before dubbing on a small pinch of cream hare's fur. Twist the fur to form a thin rope, then wind it on to form a small thorax.

6 Take a small pinch of natural deer hair and catch it in so the tips project over the eye. As with all deer hair wings, secure with tight thread turns, then apply a couple of softer controlling turns.

7 Trim away the soft hair butts to leave a short stub, then prepare a short-fibered dark gray cock hackle and catch it in at the base of the wing.

8 Using hackle pliers apply two or three turns of the hackle tight against the base of the wing. Secure the hackletip with thread and remove the excess. Wind the thread to the eye before casting it off with a secure whip finish.

See also FEATHER FIBER BODY, PAGE 24

COLLAR HACKLE, PAGE 36

Orange Hopper

Although called a hopper, this is no grasshopper imitation but a top-notch dry fly designed for use in still water, and it works superbly in a hatch of big midges. Its basic profile is that of a small crane fly or daddy longlegs but the Hopper is often tied in nonimitative colors such as orange, red, and claret.

What makes the Hopper so distinctive and effective is the trailing legs formed from strands of knotted cock pheasant tail fibers. Tying the knotted pheasant tail legs is difficult but pre-knotted legs can easily be purchased from material suppliers.

A fine pearl rib is added to give the body extra sparkle.

RECIPE

HOOK:	*Size 10–12 mediumweight wet fly*
THREAD:	*Brown*
RIB:	*Fine pearl tinsel*
BODY:	*Orange SLF or similar*
LEGS:	*Knotted fibers of cock pheasant tail*
HACKLE:	*Brown cock hackle*

1 Having fixed the hook in the vise, run the tying thread down the shank in close turns. Carry the thread a short distance around the bend and catch in 2-inch (5-cm) fine pearl tinsel.

FISH FOR:

Brown trout

Rainbow trout

2 Cover the waste end of the tinsel with turns of thread, then dub on a small pinch of orange fur to create a tapered rope. Remember to apply a touch of wax to the thread before adding the fur.

Fine pearl tinsel

When a midge is hatching at the surface, the body of the pupa has a pronounced sparkle caused by gas trapped beneath its skin. A rib of fine pearl tinsel mimics this sparkle and is a major trigger point for trout that feed on the naturals.

Orange SLF

For dry flies such as the Orange Hopper it is important that the fur used can be teased or ragged out so that light can shine through the fibers and also so it can help the fly to float. Though the original material for this fly was seal's fur substitutes such as SLF, which has a similar trilobal texture, work equally well. Avoid softer furs such as rabbit that don't work quite so well.

Cock pheasant tail

The tailfeathers of the male ring-necked pheasant not only provide a great body material for a large number of nymph and dry-fly patterns but also make great legs either for crane fly imitations or for the hopper series of stillwater dry flies. In order to create the impression of leg joints, one or two simple overhand knots are made in the fiber.

Brown cock hackle

When tying patterns designed to sit low in the surface film, use a hackle with softer fibers.

3 Starting at the point where the tinsel is fixed, wind on close turns of the dubbed fur. The effect should not be too slim as the body needs to have plenty of fibers sticking out.

4 Stop when the fur has covered three-quarters of the hook shank and a tapered body has been formed, then take hold of the pearl tinsel and wind it over the body in five evenly spaced turns.

5 Secure the loose end of the tinsel with tying thread and remove the excess. Next take a single strand of cock pheasant tail and make a single overhand knot a short distance from the tip. This forms a leg joint.

6 Repeat the process to form six legs in total, or use commercially pre-tied legs. Making sure their tips are level, tie in three legs each side of the body so they trail past the bend. Remove the waste ends with scissors.

7 Prepare a brown cock hackle and catch it in just in front of the body. Using hackle pliers, wind on three or four turns of the hackle so that it finishes just behind the eye.

8 Secure the hackletip with thread and remove the waste end. Build a small neat head and cast off the thread with a whip finish. Finally, trim away the hackle fibers on the underside of the fly so that it sits low in the water.

See also   DUBBING (SIMPLE), PAGE 28

COLLAR HACKLE, PAGE 36

Olive Midge Pupa

RECIPE

HOOK:	*Size 12–16 caddis hook*
THREAD:	*Olive*
TAIL & HEAD	*White antron yarn*
RIB:	*Silver wire*
BODY:	*Dyed olive goose herl*
WING BUDS:	*Orange goose biots*
THORAX:	*50/50 blend of olive and orange fur*
THORAX COVER:	*Dyed olive goose herl*

Trout will take midge pupae anywhere in the water column from hard on the bottom to right at the surface. This pattern is lightly dressed so that it can be fished just subsurface and imitates the pupae of medium to large species of Chironomid midge.

When fish are feeding close to the surface they become more critical of the pattern being used. For this reason the Olive Midge Pupa employs major recognition points such as the wing buds and breathing filaments at both the head and tip of the abdomen.

Though this pattern imitates olive-colored pupae it can also be tied in black and brown to imitate similarly colored species.

1 Fix the hook in the vise and run the thread well around the bend, repositioning the hook if necessary to allow access. Catch in a slim section of white antron, 2 inches (5 cm) of silver wire and a few fibers of olive goose herl.

FISH FOR:

Brown trout

Cutthroat trout

Rainbow trout

2 Draw the waste ends of all the thread materials along the hook shank and secure them with close turns of thread. This forms a slim, even base on which to apply the feather fiber body.

Dyed olive goose herl
Feather fiber makes superb bodies on both nymphs and dry flies. Goose herl is a particular favorite because the fibers are long and can be dyed a wide range of colors.

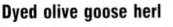

Fine silver wire
Silver wire is used here to protect the delicate feather fiber body. It also adds a little sparkle and suggests the segmentation of the pupa's abdomen.

50/50 blend of olive and orange fur
When you look at an insect closely, you see that a mixture of colors forms the overall color. Blending different colors of fur together produces a very effective result.

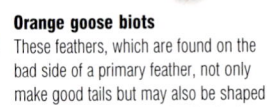

White antron yarn
Antron yarn has a wide range of uses, and in white it is very effective in suggesting the delicate filaments found at the head and tail of a midge pupa.

Orange goose biots
These feathers, which are found on the bad side of a primary feather, not only make good tails but may also be shaped to suggest a midge pupa's wing buds.

3 Gently take hold of the fibers of goose herl and begin winding them along the hook shank. Do not twist the fibers; instead, allow them to spread flat so that the body is as thin as possible.

4 When the feather fiber has covered three-quarters of the way back to the eye, secure the loose ends with thread. Wind the silver wire in evenly spaced turns applied in the opposite direction to the feather fibers.

5 Secure the loose end of the wire and remove it and the excess feather fibers. Take two orange goose biots and trim each into a round shape at the end. Catch them in either side of the body to form the wing buds.

6 Cover the waste ends of the goose biots, then catch in a second bunch of dyed olive goose fibers by their tips just in front of the body.

7 Take a short section of white antron yarn and catch it in at the eye. Secure with figure-of-eight thread wraps so that the ends stick out to the sides. Dub on a blend of olive and orange fur and wind to form the thorax.

8 Wind the thread to the eye, then draw the feather fibers between the two ends of the antron yarn. Secure the feather fibers and remove the excess. Cast off with a whip finish and trim the head and tail breathers.

See also   FEATHER FIBER BODY, PAGE 24

DUBBING (SIMPLE), PAGE 28

Sparkle Pupa

Developed by Gary LaFontaine after close study of the real thing, this pattern is now one of the best imitations of a caddis pupa.

Particularly distinctive is the way the body material is enveloped in a loose shuck, a method that allows the fly to hold bubbles of air and that produces a very natural effect.

Tying in strands of antron yarn over the top and bottom of a dubbed body creates the envelope. This yarn should never be pulled tight but instead allowed to billow out around the body, a profile that can be enhanced by easing the fibers around the sides of the body before they are finally secured.

RECIPE

HOOK:	*Size 12–16 wet fly*
THREAD:	*Yellow*
TAIL:	*Yellow antron yarn*
BODY:	*Amber fur and pearl Lite Brite*
BODY COVER:	*Yellow antron yarn*
WING:	*Natural deer hair*
THORAX:	*Hare's fur*

1 Fix the hook in the vise and run the thread down the shank to a point opposite the barb. Remove approximately one-third the diameter of a length of antron yarn and catch it in as a tail.

FISH FOR:

Brown trout

Rainbow trout

Cutthroat

2 Take another length of antron yarn and split it down the middle so that it is half the thickness. Catch in one-half on top of the shank at the same point as the tail.

Natural deer hair
A pinch of deer hair suggests the legs and expanding wings of the emerging caddis fly.

Hare's fur
The mottled browns of hare's fur are used here to suggest the darker thorax area of the caddis pupa.

Yellow antron yarn
This sparkling man-made product can be used in strands or applied as a dubbing. Yellow is used here to imitate a small, amber-colored caddis pupa, but green, gray, and cream also work well.

Pearl Lite Brite and Amber fur
Though the body of the original was plain fur, blending it with a touch of pearl Lite Brite can enhance the effect.

3 Take the other half of the split antron yarn and catch it in at a point corresponding to the first but this time beneath the hook shank. If access is a problem invert the hook in the vise.

4 Take a pinch of amber yellow dubbing and blend it with 30 percent of pearl Lite Brite. Dub this onto the tying thread, covering the waste ends of the antron yarn, to form a chunky body.

5 Draw the antron yarn loosely over the top of the body and secure so that a small loop forms. If necessary, use the point of a needle to prevent the loop from closing.

6 Repeat the process with the lower strand of the yarn. That done, ease the fibers of antron around the body so that they form a loose envelope.

7 Secure the antron with further thread wraps, then trim off the excess. Select a few well-marked deer hairs and catch them in to make a short wing. Fix them with tight thread wraps, adding a couple of softer turns to stop them from flaring.

8 Trim away the excess deer hair and cover the ends with thread. Finally, dub on a small pinch of natural hare's fur and wind it on to form the head. Cast off the thread with a whip finish.

See also   HAIRWING, PAGE 26

DUBBING (SIMPLE), PAGE 28

Red Quill

HOOK:	*Size 14–20 dry fly*
THREAD:	*Brown*
TAIL:	*Brown cock hackle fibers*
BODY:	*Stripped peacock eye quill*
WING:	*Natural gray CDC*
HACKLE:	*Brown cock hackle fibers*

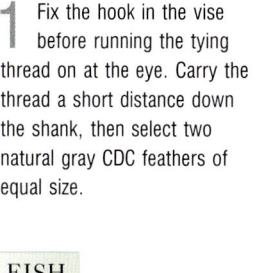

The name Red Quill derives from the reddish brown coloration of the hackles and the body of stripped peacock quill. The fly itself has a long pedigree and may be tied either as wet or dry.

In the original the wing was either omitted or comprised slips of starling or mallard primary, but here it is the now ubiquitous but very effective CDC. CDC works well and is a lot easier to tie than paired wings.

The material for the body comes from a peacock's eye feather. With the flue removed, this quill produces a segmented effect when wound over the hook.

1 Fix the hook in the vise before running the tying thread on at the eye. Carry the thread a short distance down the shank, then select two natural gray CDC feathers of equal size.

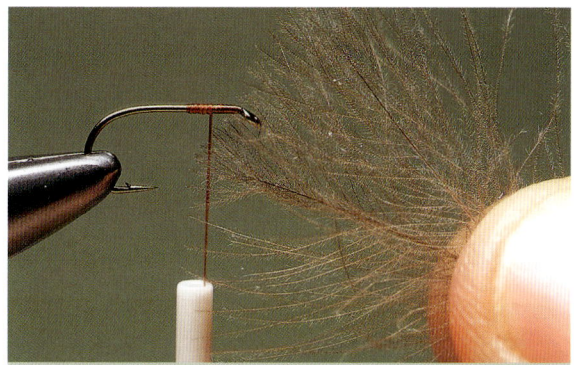

FISH FOR:

Brown trout

Rainbow trout

2 Place the feathers so that the tips are level and catch them in with tight thread turns. They should project over the eye. When tied in, these tips should be a little longer than the hook shank.

Stripped peacock eye quill
Though stripped hackle stems may be used, peacock eye feather produces a better if less robust effect. Using an eraser and fingernail to remove the entire flue is the best solution, albeit a rather tedious method.

Natural CDC
Again, natural gray CDC makes a great substitute for paired feather slips, being much easier to apply and, if anything, even more effective.

Brown cock hackle fibers
Choose hackles with a nice reddish brown hue. For tying the Red Quill as a dry fly these should be either top-quality neck or saddle feathers.

3 Prepare a brown cock hackle and catch it in at the rear of the wing. Secure the hackle stem with close thread turns and remove the excess material. Carry the thread down the shank to form a smooth tapered base.

4 At the bend catch in a few fibers of brown cock hackle as a tail. Add further thread turns to even up the transition from tail to body.

5 Take a single strand from a peacock eye quill and strip away the flue with a fingernail. Any that remains can be removed with a soft rubber eraser, which is best used on a hard, smooth surface.

6 Catch in the stripped quill at the base of the tail. Carry the thread back up to the wing, counterwinding so that it flattens, helping to form a smooth, tapered base for the body.

7 Take hold of the quill and wind it carefully along the hook. Make sure that the turns are closely butted together and that no gaps form. It is also important that they don't overlap so the segmented effect is nice and even.

8 Secure the end of the quill with thread and remove the excess. Use a couple of turns in front of the wing to bring it to an upright position, then wind on close turns of hackle behind and in front of the wing.

See also COLLAR HACKLE, PAGE 36

GE Nymph

RECIPE

HOOK:	*Size 14–20*
THREAD:	*Olive*
TAIL:	*Olive CDC*
RIB:	*Clear nylon monofilament*
BODY:	*Olive CDC*
WING CASES:	*Natural gray CDC*
THORAX:	*Olive CDC*

The GE, or General Emerger, Nymph imitates a variety of small mayflies at the point of emerging from their nymphal stage. The entire pattern is tied from CDC, a soft downy feather that is usually used as a wing but may also be dubbed to form a body or thorax. By allowing some of the fibers to stick out, the general buzz of an emerging insect is suggested, and it helps the fly float.

For the wing cases CDC fibers are tied in a loop or bubble-back that imitates the bulge of an emerging insect's wings and also traps a bubble of air, again helping the fly float. When tying this wing style, a needle tip will help to achieve the right profile.

1 Having fixed the hook in the vise, run on the tying thread at the eye. Carry it down to the bend in close turns before catching in a few fibers of dyed olive CDC as the tail.

FISH FOR:

Brown trout

Cutthroat

Rainbow trout

2 Catch in 2 inches (5 cm) of fine, clear nylon monofilament at the tail base before securing the waste end to the shank with turns of thread. Tear off a pinch of olive CDC and dub it onto the thread.

Clear nylon monofilament
Where the addition of extra weight
is not appropriate as in sparse,
no-hackle flies, clear nylon or
fluorocarbon monofilament is
a perfect ribbing material.

Natural gray CDC
Natural CDC, with its fine downy texture
and surface-grabbing fibers, is ideal for
suggesting the
emerging wings of
a small mayfly or
midge.

Olive CDC
Though natural CDC feathers are
basically gray or white, the latter may be
dyed a wide range of colors. As well as
being suitable for wings and tail, CDC
also makes great dubbed bodies on dry
flies and emergers.

3 Starting at the base of the tail, wind on the dubbed CDC to form a slim, slightly tapered body.

4 When the dubbed body has been applied so that it covers two thirds of the hook shank, take hold of the clear nylon monofilament and apply it in open, evenly spaced turns.

5 Secure the loose end of the monofilament with thread and remove the excess. Next, take a good pinch of gray CDC fibers and catch them in by their butts immediately in front of the body.

6 Tear off another pinch of the same olive CDC as used for the body and dub that onto the tying thread. Wind it over the butts of the gray CDC to form a small but pronounced thorax.

7 With the tying thread now positioned at the eye, draw the gray CDC over the back of the thorax. Do not draw tight; you need to create a noticeable hump. Using the tip of a needle can help achieve this more easily.

8 Finally, secure the gray CDC at the eye with a few tight thread turns. Cast off the thread with a whip finish before pinching off any stray fibers of CDC with a thumbnail.

See also   DUBBING (SIMPLE), PAGE 28

Baetis Nymph

A thin, flexible plastic tube adds a wonderful translucency to any nymph pattern as well as providing a lifelike segmentation. Materials such as Ultra Lace work well on patterns such as this Baetis Nymph, which imitates a number of small, olive-colored mayfly nymphs.

The downside of plastics is that they can produce a hard, lifeless silhouette unless combined with softer, livelier materials.

Here, rather than being wound, the partridge hackle is cut into a V shape and applied over the top of the thorax. The technique works well for medium to large nymphs but on very small patterns it may be dispensed with.

RECIPE

HOOK:	*Size 14–18 wet fly*
THREAD:	*Gray*
TAIL:	*Dyed olive partridge*
BODY:	*Olive Ultra Lace*
HACKLE:	*Dyed olive partridge*
THORAX:	*Dyed olive hare's fur*
THORAX COVER:	*Brown or olive plastic strip*

1 Fix the hook in the vise and run the thread in close turns down to the hook bend. There, catch in a few fibers of olive partridge. Take the thread three-quarters of the way back up the hook shank and catch in a length of olive Ultra Lace.

FISH FOR:

Brown trout

Cutthroat

Rainbow trout

2 Add a few more tight thread turns, then stretch the olive Ultra Lace along the hook shank, securing it in place with further close turns of thread. Stretching the Ultra Lace reduces its bulk.

Olive Ultra Lace
Ultra Lace is a thin, flexible tube available in a wide range of colors. It may be used either as a rib or wound in close turns to form the entire body of either nymphs or larval patterns. It should always be wound under tension and stretched thin to provide maximum translucence.

Brown or olive plastic strip
Flexible plastic strips including products such as Magic Shrimp or Scud Back work like a skin, encasing the body of shrimp and caddis patterns, and are also used to form the thorax cover on a range of nymph patterns.

Dyed olive partridge
Like hare's fur the natural color of partridge feathers is basically a speckled brown. For this reason the two materials complement each other perfectly. They also work well when dyed. In this pattern the partridge is dyed olive and mimics all manner of small, olive-colored mayfly nymphs.

Dyed olive hare's fur
In its natural state hare's fur has a subtle, mottled brown color that makes it a wonderful material for tying a variety of imitative and suggestive patterns. Dying it a range of colors, including olive, increases its uses still further.

3 When the thread has reached the tail, wind it back to the point at which the Ultra Lace was caught in, then begin winding it in close turns. Tension should be applied to Ultra Lace at all times while it is being wound.

4 Continue winding the Ultra Lace along the shank until it has reached the tying thread. The body should be slim with a segmented effect. Secure the loose end of the Ultra Lace and remove the excess.

5 Take a short length of brown or olive plastic strip and catch it in, shiny side up, on top of the last turn of the body material.

6 Dub on a small pinch of dyed olive hare's fur and wind on to form the thorax. Next take a small dyed olive partridge feather and strip away the base fibers before removing the tip with scissors.

7 Take the V-shaped section of partridge feather and catch it in by its bare stem at the eye so that it sits on top of the thorax. Pull in gently until the point of the V is just over the thorax.

8 Draw the plastic strip over the back of the thorax at the same time, stretching it slightly. Secure it at the eye with thread turns. Remove the excess strip and feather stem and build a small head, then cast off the thread.

See also   RIBBING SET, PAGE 22

DUBBING (SIMPLE), PAGE 28

Golden Olive Bumble

RECIPE

HOOK:	*Size 8–12 wet fly*
THREAD:	*Brown*
TAIL:	*Golden pheasant topping*
RIB:	*Fine oval gold tinsel*
BODY:	*Golden olive seal's fur*
BODY HACKLE:	*Brown and golden olive cock hackles*
COLLAR HACKLE:	*Blue jay or dyed blue guinea fowl*

This is a traditional Irish Lough fly—part of Kingsmill Moore's Bumble series, which includes the very popular Claret Bumble. The name Bumble derives from the effect the double hackle creates. Employing a technique known as "palmering," these hackles are wound along the body forming a fly that creates a lot of disturbance in the water.

Setting off the golden olive body is a ruff of blue jay, a feather notoriously difficult to work with, especially when trying to produce a collar hackle. The original method was to split the quill before winding it on. This method is much easier.

1 Run the tying thread on at the eye, carrying it down the shank in close turns. Select a small, well-colored golden pheasant topping feather and catch it in at a point opposite the hook barb.

FISH FOR:

Brown trout

Rainbow trout

2 With the topping positioned with a nice upward curve, secure it in place with a couple of tight thread turns. Next catch in 2-inch (5-cm) fine oval gold tinsel at the tail base.

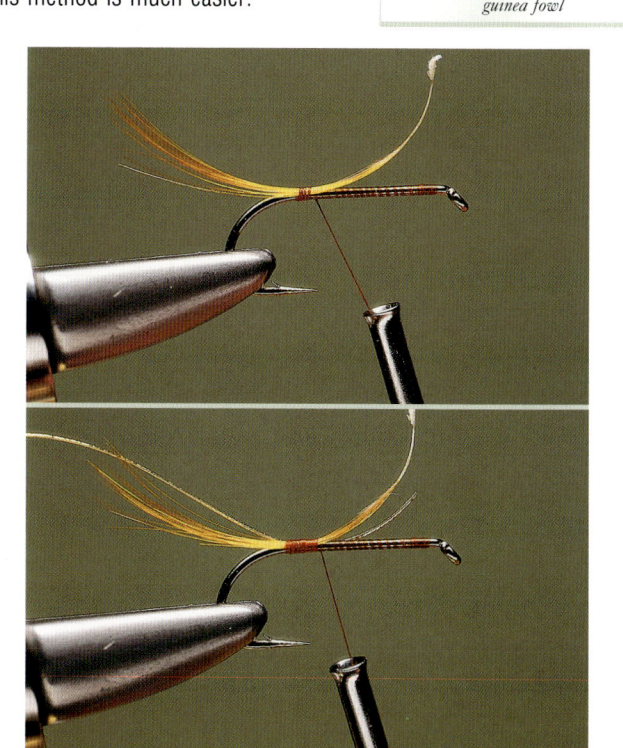

Golden pheasant topping

"Topping" is the term used for the translucent, golden yellow crest feathers of the golden pheasant. They are used for a large number of traditional wet flies and Atlantic salmon patterns.

Brown cock hackles

Used in conjunction with golden olive hackles, brown cock hackles produce a dense water-moving effect when palmered the full length of the body.

Blue jay

This bright blue and black barred feather comes from the wing of a European jay. Not always easy to obtain, dyed blue guinea fowl is a perfectly acceptable alternative.

Golden olive seal's fur

In reality, this fur is almost yellow with just a hint of olive. Though a substitute may be used, real seal's fur has a beautiful translucency.

Golden olive cock hackles

This color hackle is used in few other patterns but is a definite must for the Golden Olive Bumble.

Oval gold tinsel

Oval gold tinsel adds a sparkle to any fly, and in this case is used also to lock the turns of hackle securely to the body.

3 Secure the waste ends of the topping and the tinsel along the shank with close thread turns before removing the excess. Dub on a generous pinch of golden olive seal's fur and wind on to form a thick, quite ragged body.

4 Stop the body a short distance from the eye before selecting two cock hackles—one brown, the other dyed golden olive. These should both have a fiber length nearly twice that of the hook gape.

5 Prepare the hackles by removing the soft fibers at their base before catching them in just in front of the body. Grasp both hackles at the same time and wind down the body in open, evenly spaced turns.

6 Continue winding on the hackles, making sure that they do not separate, until they have reached the tail. Retaining tension on them with the hackle pliers, begin to wind the oval tinsel up through the hackles in evenly spaced turns.

7 Secure the tinsel at the eye and remove the excess plus the hackletips. Next, tear off a bunch of blue jay hackle fibers and trim the butts so that they are level. Catch the bunch in so the tips project over the eye.

8 Allow the blue jay fibers to spin evenly around the shank, then fold them back over the body so that they form a collar. Secure them with turns of thread before building a neat head and casting off with a whip finish.

See also   DUBBING (SIMPLE), PAGE 28

March Brown

RECIPE

HOOK:	*Size 10–14 wet fly*
THREAD:	*Brown*
TAIL:	*Brown partridge fibers*
RIB:	*Yellow thread*
BODY:	*Hare's fur*
WING:	*Hen pheasant wing*
HACKLE:	*Brown partridge*

This fly was originally tied to represent a large dark mayfly of the same name that hatches out during early spring. The hackle and tail material comes from the plumage of the gray or English partridge. This bird has a wonderful mottling to its feathers, which range from a fine speckled gray to brown, making them ideal for suggesting an insect's legs.

Today, the pattern is most often used as a general pattern, the natural colors making it far more versatile than simply the imitation of one insect species. It is also tied as the Silver March Brown, which substitutes silver tinsel for the hare's fur body.

1 Fix the hook in the vise and run the tying thread down to the bend. Tear off three or four fibers of brown partridge hackle and, using two or three thread wraps, catch them in at the bend to form the tail.

FISH FOR:

Brown trout

Rainbow trout

2 Secure the partridge fibers so the tail is about the same length as the hook shank. Catch in 2 inches (5 cm) of yellow thread at the tail base, allowing the waste end to lie along the shank.

Hare's fur

The mottled brown tones of hare's body fur works well in a whole range of wet flies and nymphs. Ragging it out after dubbing allows all the guard hairs to give the finished fly a natural-looking buzz.

Hen pheasant wing quills

These feathers exhibit a range of browns and creams that work well for the wings of caddis patterns as well as imitations of the larger, darker species of mayfly such as the March Brown.

Yellow thread

Yellow tying thread is the preferred material for ribbing this classic wet fly pattern, however, yellow wire or oval gold tinsel work equally well and are tougher, too.

Brown partridge hackles

The fine black and brown speckling found in brown partridge hackles creates a very lifelike effect suggesting the legs of either a nymph or adult insect.

3 Cover the waste ends of the yellow thread and tail material with close turns of thread. Trim away any material ends that come close to the eye, then apply a small pinch of hare's fur onto the threads.

4 Using a simple finger-and-thumb twist, dub the fur onto the thread to form an even rope that tapers to a point. Wind this in close turns along the hook shank to form the body.

5 Continue winding the fur until it has reached a point just short of the eye. Remove any excess fur, then take the yellow thread and wind it along the body in evenly spaced turns.

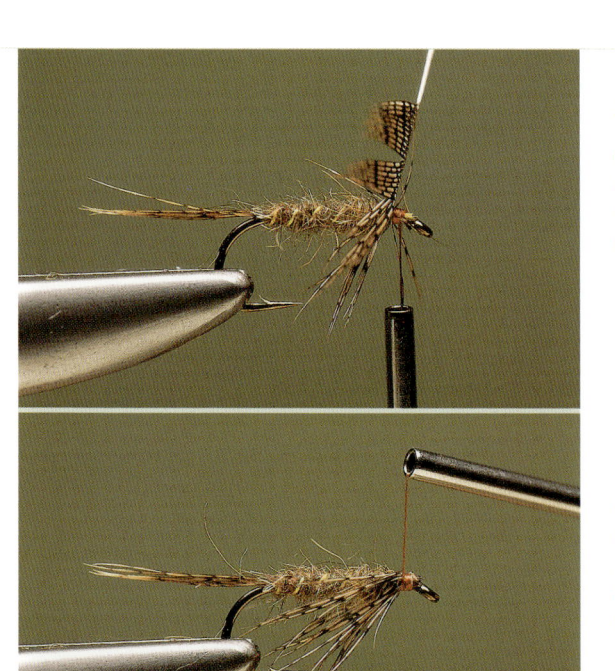

6 Secure the loose end of the ribbing thread and remove the excess. Catch in a small brown partridge feather, by its tip, and wind on three turns to form the hackle.

7 Secure the hackle with thread turns and remove the excess. Stroke the hackle fibers back so that they sit along the sides and beneath the body. Fix them in position with two or three more thread wraps.

8 Take a pair of hen pheasant wing quills and remove a thin slip from each feather. Place the matching slips together so their tips are level, and position with a winging loop. Secure with further thread turns, having first removed the excess material.

See also   DUBBING (SIMPLE), PAGE 28

PAIRED WING—SOFT LOOP, PAGE 40

Silver Invicta

This is the silver-bodied version of the Invicta, a classic winged wet fly used primarily on lakes. The original Invicta has a body of yellow fur, making it an effective pattern when trout are taking caddis pupae, while the slimmer, sparkling body of this works well when they are feeding on midges or even small fish.

When tying a throat or false hackle, it is important that the fibers flare around the sides of the body. Some tiers find this easier to achieve if the hook is first inverted on the vise. Once the fibers are caught in with a couple of thread wraps, they are correctly positioned with the fingers before being secured.

RECIPE

HOOK:	*Size 8–14 mediumweight wet fly*
THREAD:	*Brown or black*
TAIL:	*Pheasant topping*
RIB:	*Fine oval silver tinsel*
BODY:	*Flat silver tinsel*
BODY HACKLE:	*Brown cock hackle*
WING:	*Hen pheasant center tail*
THROAT HACKLE:	*Dyed blue guinea fowl*

1 Fix the hook in the vise and run the tying thread down the shank to a point opposite the barb. There catch in a small golden pheasant topping plus 2 inches (5 cm) of fine oval silver tinsel.

FISH FOR:

Brown trout

Rainbow trout

2 Wind close turns of thread along the hook shank covering the waste ends of the tail and ribbing materials. Cut one end of a length of flat, silver mylar to a point and catch it near the eye.

Golden pheasant topping

This translucent golden yellow comes from the crest of the golden pheasant and is used widely in many traditional wet flies and Atlantic salmon flies.

Flat silver tinsel

Originally, real metal was used when a smooth sparkling body was required. While it is still possible to obtain this material, it has now mostly been superseded by mylar-based products that, being plastic-based, are easier to work with and retain their shine indefinitely.

Brown cock hackle

A brown cock hackle is used to add a buzz to the Silver Invicta. Choose one with soft fibers to add movement to the fly.

Oval silver tinsel

Oval tinsel is available in a variety of diameters and in two main colors: gold and silver. It is used in many traditional wet fly patterns both to add sparkle and to protect body materials and hackles.

Dyed blue guinea fowl

Blue jay feathers are the material originally used for the throat hackle of the Silver Invicta. As the genuine article is often difficult to obtain, a reasonable substitute can be made by using dyed blue guinea fowl feathers.

Hen pheasant center tail

This is not an easy material to work with but has a beautiful texture of mottled brown, gray, and black. Because the fibers are prone to splitting, look for fresh, top-quality feathers that are not dry and brittle.

3 Wind the flat, silver mylar tinsel down the shank in close, but not overlapping, turns. When the tail base has been reached, wind the tinsel back over itself to form a double layer.

4 Secure the loose end of the tinsel, then remove the excess. Select and prepare a brown cock hackle with soft fibers approximately one-and-a-half times longer than the hook gape. Catch in and apply in evenly spaced turns.

5 Wind the hackle until it has reached the tail. Retaining tension on the hackle, wind the oval tinsel up through it in evenly spaced turns. Wiggling the tinsel on each turn will stop any hackle fibers from becoming trapped.

6 Secure the loose end of the tinsel and remove both it and the excess hackletip. Next, catch in a few fibers of dyed blue guinea fowl, as here, to form a beard hackle. Inverting the hook will help many tiers with this process.

7 Return the hook to its original position in the vise. Taking a hen pheasant center tailfeather, remove a slip approximately three times greater in size than the intended wing. Stroke the fibers so the tips are level and the fibers marry.

8 Fold one end of the slip to its middle, then fold again to create a rolled wing. Catch this in at the eye with a couple of winging loops, then secure with tight turns. Remove the excess feather, build a neat head, and cast off.

See also   PAIRED WING—SOFT LOOP, PAGE 40

TINSEL BODY, PAGE 42

Fiery Brown

RECIPE

HOOK:	*Size 8–12 mediumweight wet fly*
THREAD:	*Brown*
TAIL:	*Golden pheasant tippets*
RIB:	*Fine oval gold tinsel*
BODY:	*Fiery brown seal's fur or substitute*
WING:	*Brown mallard*
HACKLE:	*Brown cock hackle*

The Fiery Brown works best on the large limestone loughs of Ireland, having been developed from a traditional Irish salmon fly.

It is said to be a representation of a freshwater shrimp, and is most effective when fished as the point fly of a three-fly cast.

This pattern uses a combination of gold tinsel and seal's fur to add translucence to an otherwise solid silhouette. This is achieved by tying the body thick and full, then teasing out the fibers with the tip of a dubbing needle or a piece of Velcro. Allowing the tinsel ribbing to bed into the fur means the sparkle it produces appears to come from within the body.

1 With the hook fixed in the vise, run the tying thread on at the eye and wind it down to the bend in close turns. Tear off a few fibers of golden pheasant tippets and catch them in at a point opposite the barb.

FISH FOR:

Brown trout

2 Take 2 inches (5 cm) of fine, oval gold tinsel, and, using a couple of tight thread turns, catch this in at the same point as the tail. This tinsel should sit on the far side of the hook shank.

Golden pheasant tippets
These striking orange and black feathers come from the cape of the golden pheasant. They are used in both the tail and wings of a range of traditional wet flies and Atlantic salmon flies.

Brown mallard shoulder
This brown speckled feather is used in many traditional wet flies, most notably those in the mallard series. It can be difficult to obtain but dyed gray mallard flank is an acceptable substitute.

Brown cock hackle
This is used to suggest legs, but also to add mobility. Cock hackles with soft, webby fibers are best for this type of fly.

Oval gold tinsel
Here, the oval gold tinsel is used to add sparkle to the fur body.

Fiery brown seal's fur
Seal's fur dyed a rich fiery brown is the traditional material for the body of this fly, adding a wonderful sparkle and translucence. Good substitutes are available but choose one with a trilobal construction that is similar to the texture of the real thing.

3 Using close turns of tying thread, secure the waste ends of the tail and ribbing material to the hook shank before trimming off any excess with scissors. Apply a body of dubbed seal's fur, having first waxed the thread.

4 Continue winding on the dubbed fur until it has reached a point a short distance from the eye, remembering to leave enough space for the wing and hackle. Wind on the gold tinsel in open, evenly spaced turns.

5 Select a soft-fibered brown cock hackle. This should have a fiber length slightly greater than the hook gape. Prepare it and catch it in just in front of the body.

6 Grasp the tip of the hackle with hackle pliers and wind on three full turns. Secure the hackletip with thread before trimming off the excess. Stroke the fibers back over the body and position with a couple of thread turns.

7 Take a slip of well-marked brown mallard shoulder three times the width of the intended wing. Fold one edge into the middle of the slip, then fold it again to create a rolled wing.

8 Position the slip so its tip extends as far as the tail and fix with a couple of winging loops. Once in position, add further tight turns and remove any excess material at the eye. Finally, cast off with a whip finish.

See also   RIBBING SET, PAGE 22

DUBBING (SIMPLE), PAGE 28

Hot Butt Caddis

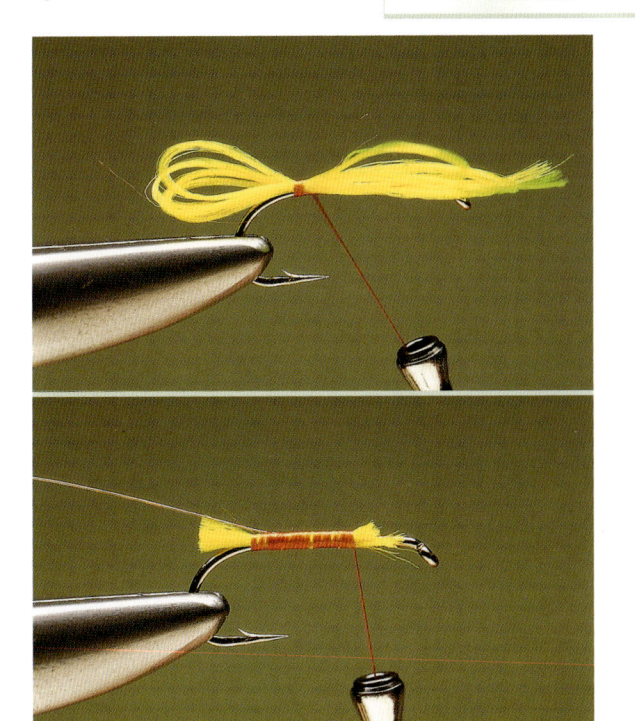

This is a version of the ever-popular Elk Hair Caddis, a deadly dry fly wherever small to medium-sized caddis flies hatch. Using fluorescent materials to add punch to a subtly hued fly is a well-established technique—even when tying imitative patterns. Here the fluorescent floss is added in two ways. The first is as a short tail or butt, the second by blending natural hare's fur with the same tail material chopped fine.

While it is easy to obtain preblended furs that contain fluorescent colors, it is a simple matter to create your own using waste material cut into short lengths.

RECIPE

HOOK: *Size 10–14 mediumweight dry fly*

THREAD: *Brown*

TAIL: *Fluorescent chartreuse floss*

RIB: *Fine gold wire*

BODY: *A blend of hare's fur and chopped fluorescent floss—ratio 3:1*

WING: *Tan elk hock*

HACKLE: *Furnace cock saddle hackle*

1 Fix the hook in the vise and run the thread down to the bend. Take a length of fluorescent chartreuse floss and fold three times to create eight strands. Catch in the floss at a point opposite the barb.

FISH FOR:

Brown trout

Cutthroat

Rainbow trout

2 Catch in 2-inch (5-cm) fine gold wire on the far side of the hook, covering the waste ends of wire and floss with close turns of thread. Remove the excess floss with scissors.

Fluorescent floss
This type of floss comes in a wide range of bright colors. Chartreuse or lime green work well in this pattern but orange and red are also worth trying.

Elk hock
This is a tough, short-fibered hair found on an elk's lower leg. It is hollow at its base, providing a degree of buoyancy—ideal for winging dry flies. It is available either as natural, bleached, or dyed a range of colors.

Furnace saddle hackles
Saddle hackles have a wonderfully even fiber length along the entire stem. This makes them perfect for tying dry flies with body or palmered hackles. The natural furnace color is brown with a black center.

Gold wire
Fine gold wire makes a tough practical ribbing material on a variety of medium-sized dry flies. Here it not only fixes the body hackle in place but also adds a little sparkle.

Hare's fur
The subtle shades of brown found in natural hare's fur make great bodies on a whole variety of dry flies and nymphs. Mix the soft underfur with a few of the stiffer guard hairs to produce a blend that dubs well but still looks buglike.

3 Take a pinch of natural hare's fur and mix it with a small amount of the waste floss that has been chopped into short lengths. Apply this to prewaxed thread.

4 Using a finger-and-thumb twist, dub the fur into a rope and wind this along the shank in close turns to form the body. Make sure that the turns are even and that there are no gaps.

5 Prepare a furnace saddle hackle before catching it in at the front of the body. Using hackle pliers, take hold of the hackle by its tip, and wind it in two close turns followed by further openly spaced turns.

6 When the hackle has reached the base of the tail, take the gold wire and wind it up through the hackle. Do not remove the hackle pliers at this point. Secure the loose end of the wire and remove the excess.

7 Trim away the excess hackletip with scissors, then remove a bunch of elk hair from the skin. Using two thread turns, position the hair on top of the body so the tips project just past the bend.

8 Add tight thread turns to secure the hair, then, to counteract the flaring effect of the tight thread, add a couple of looser turns to position the hair low over the body. Cast off with a whip finish and trim the hair butts.

See also   HAIRWING, PAGE 26

DUBBING (SIMPLE), PAGE 28

High-sight Parachute Adams

RECIPE

HOOK:	*Size 10–22 dry fly*
THREAD:	*White*
TAIL:	*Grizzly and brown cock hackle fibers*
BODY:	*Muskrat or gray rabbit underfur*
WING POST:	*Orange foam dowel*
HACKLE:	*Grizzly and brown cock hackles*
THORAX:	*Muskrat or gray rabbit*

This is the parachute-style tying of the Adams, a pattern that has become the classic modern dry fly. It incorporates the same shades of gray and brown that made the original so deadly, but instead of hackletip wings it uses a wing post around which the hackle is wound.

The wing post can be constructed from a variety of materials from calf tail to polypropylene yarn or, as here, buoyant microcellular foam. The beauty of foam is that it not only helps the fly to float but if a highly colored type is used, it makes a great indicator, allowing the fly's path to be followed as it drifts downstream sitting low in the surface film.

1 Build a bed of close turns of thread one-third of the hook shank's length back from the eye. Fix a short length of foam dowel in place with further thread turns around its base to bring it to an upright position.

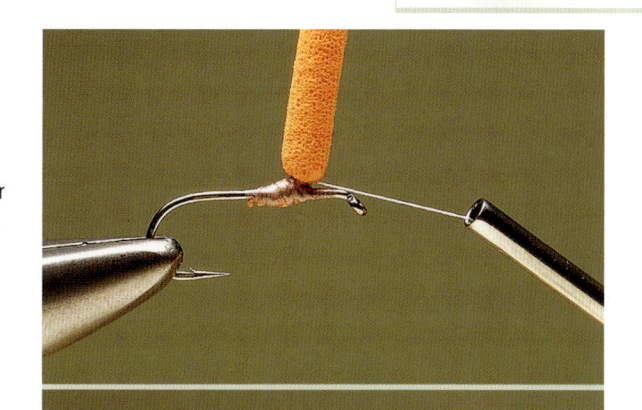

FISH FOR:

Brown trout

Rainbow trout

Cutthroat

2 Carry the tying thread down to the hook bend in close turns. Tear a few fibers from brown and grizzly cock hackles and place the fibers together, tips level. Catch in at a point opposite the barb.

Grizzly and brown cock hackles

Mixing grizzly and brown cock hackles together produces a super effect that is the hallmark of the Adams in all its guises. It is a combination that also works well in other similar dry flies.

Orange foam posts

Orange foam posts are both light and highly visible. This makes them very useful on patterns that sit low in the water and are otherwise difficult to see. They help the fly to float, too.

Rabbit fur

The original Adams uses muskrat fur. If you can obtain it, fine, but if you can't use the dark gray underfur of the rabbit with just a few of the stiffer guard hairs mixed into the blend.

3 Secure the hackle fibers in place then apply a body of dubbed muskrat or gray rabbit underfur. Next, select two hackles of identical fiber length—one brown, one grizzly. Flaring the hackle allows the fiber length to be gauged.

4 Strip the soft fibers from the base of both hackles before trimming the bare stem to leave a short stub. Place them together, one on top of the other, and catch them in at the base of the wing post by the short section of bare stem.

5 Secure the hackles with further thread turns before taking the thread up to the eye. Dub on a small pinch of the same fur used for the body and wind it from the eye to the wing post to form the thorax.

6 With the thorax in place, grasp the hackletips with hackle pliers and apply three turns. Wind the hackles so that the last turn is applied close to the body and is positioned underneath the previous turns.

7 Retaining tension on the hackles with the hackle pliers, secure the loose tips with turns of tying thread. Make sure that the thread traps none of the fibers forming the hackle. Wiggling the thread as it is wound will help this to happen.

8 When the hackles are secured, cast off the tying thread with a whip finish, then carefully remove the excess hackletips with fine-pointed scissors. Finally, trim the wing post to length.

See also   PARACHUTE HACKLE, PAGE 18

DUBBING (SIMPLE), PAGE 28

Royal Wulff

The gaudiest of all the Wulff patterns, this fly still manages to tempt even the wiliest of fish. Like others in the series, the Royal Wulff has a hairwing, tied in a V shape. This makes the fly extremely tough and when combined with a close wound collar hackle, allows it to ride high even in fast, broken water.

The main problem with this style of wing is preventing the fly from becoming too bulky, especially in the smaller sizes. The remedy is to tie the wing in first tapering the waste ends before adding the body.

RECIPE

HOOK:	*Size 8–14 mediumweight hook*
THREAD:	*Brown or black*
TAIL:	*Natural deer hair or brown bucktail*
BODY:	*Peacock herl and red floss*
WING:	*White calf tail*
HACKLE:	*Brown cock hackle*

1 Fix the hook in the vise and run on a solid bed of thread one-third of the shank length from the eye. Take a bunch of calf tail and, making sure the tips are level, catch it in so it projects over the hook eye.

FISH FOR:

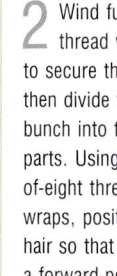

Brown trout

Cutthroat

Rainbow trout

2 Wind further thread wraps to secure the hair, then divide the bunch into two parts. Using figure-of-eight thread wraps, position the hair so that it forms a forward-pointing V shape.

Red floss

Combining red floss with peacock herl produces an effect that is attractive to fish and anglers alike.

White calf tail

This fine translucent hair is available either in plain white or in a variety of dyed colors. Its texture makes it ideal for tying a whole range of hairwinged dry flies such as the Wulff and the Trude.

Peacock herl

Any pattern that has iridescent peacock herl in its recipe is bound to be effective. The Royal Wulff is no exception.

Brown cock hackle

This pattern is designed to float high so choose a top-quality cock hackle either from the neck or saddle. For big patterns that require plenty of hackle turns, opt for the longer saddle hackle.

Natural deer hair

As an alternative to brown bucktail tips of undyed deer hair work well for this pattern being robust, the right color, and also helping the fly to float.

3 Using the scissors at an angle, trim the waste ends of the hair so that they form a taper. Prepare a brown cock saddle hackle and catch it in immediately to the rear of the wing.

4 Wind close turns of thread over the ends of the hair, then remove the excess hackle stem. Carry the thread down to the bend at this point, catching in a small bunch of natural brown deer hair as a tail.

5 Select two or three strands of peacock herl and catch them in by their tips in front of the tail. Twist gently together and wind to form a short butt.

6 Secure the ends of the herls and remove before taking the thread up the shank. Catch in 2 inches (5 cm) of red floss a short distance from the wing and wind it down to the peacock herl and back.

7 Once the central body section has been wound, secure and remove the waste end of floss. Reattach the peacock herls that were previously removed and wind on to form the front section of the body.

8 Secure the loose ends of the herls with thread and remove the excess. Take hold of the hackle by its tip and wind on close turns first behind and then in front of the wing. Secure at the eye and remove the waste.

See also	COLLAR HACKLE, PAGE 36
	FLOSS BODY, PAGE 44

X-Stimulator

If you need a big dry fly for all occasions, this is the one. Randall Kaufmann's Stimulator has a profile that can be used to suggest anything from a caddis fly to a stonefly to a grasshopper.

It is a buoyant fly, achieved by using turns of hackle running the length of the body and thorax plus bunches of elk hair for the wing and tail. Being soft and compressible, elk hair needs first to be attached using tight thread turns after which softer controlling turns are applied to the base of the tail and wing to stop the hair from flaring. The Stimulator may also be tied using rubber legs.

RECIPE

HOOK:	*Size 6–14 longshank or Living Larva hook*
THREAD:	*Fluorescent red*
TAIL AND WING:	*Natural elk hair*
RIB:	*Fine gold wire*
BODY:	*Yellow Antron*
BODY HACKLE:	*Furnace cock saddle hackle*
THORAX HACKLE:	*Grizzly cock hackle*
THORAX:	*Orange fur*
LEGS:	*Rubber strands*

1 Fix the hook in the vise and run the thread down the shank to a point opposite the barb. There, catch in a bunch of natural tan elk hair, allowing the tips to project past the bend to form the tail.

FISH FOR:

Brown trout

Cutthroat

Rainbow trout

2 Secure with tight turns, then apply close turns over the waste ends to form an even base. Take the thread back to the tail base and apply a couple of soft turns. Catch in a length of gold wire.

Natural elk hair
This fly must float high in fast and broken water, so elk hair is the perfect choice. It is buoyant and offers the right profile for imitating the wing of a large insect.

Yellow Antron
Being man-made, and less absorbent than some natural furs, Antron or SLF are the perfect choice for most types of dry fly. They are available in a range of bright and more imitative colors.

Furnace cock saddle hackle
For body hackles on big flies, saddle hackle works better than ordinary neck hackle because it is longer and of a more consistent fiber.

Orange fur
When used for the thorax, this fur, like the yellow fur used for the body, needs to be light and quick to shed water. Antron or SLF again are the perfect choice.

Fine gold wire
On big, buoyant dry flies such as the Stimulator, a wire rib protects the body and adds a touch of sparkle without affecting the ability of the fly to float.

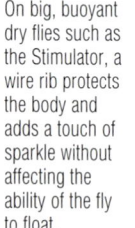

Grizzly cock hackle
The speckling of a grizzly cock hackle suggests the general buzz of an insect moving on the water's surface.

3 Apply a light coating of
wax to the thread, then
dub on a large pinch of yellow
fur. Having created a thin,
tapered rope, wind this in
close turns from the tail base
so that two-thirds of the hook
shank is covered.

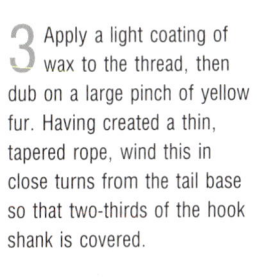

4 With the dubbed body
complete, prepare and
catch in a brown or furnace
cock saddle hackle. Take hold
of the hackle tip with hackle
pliers and wind it down to the
tail in five or six open, evenly
spaced turns.

5 Wind the gold wire rib up
through the hackle to lock
it in place before removing the
excess hackletip and wire. Next,
take a bunch of long, natural elk
hair and catch it in so the tips
reach those of the tail.

6 Secure the wing with tight thread turns, then apply a couple of soft controlling turns at the wing base. That done, take two white rubber strands and catch one in either side of the wing.

7 Prepare a grizzly cock hackle with a fiber length approximately one-and-a-half times that of the hook gape. Catch it in at the base of the wing before dubbing on a pinch of orange fur, then dub this onto the thread and apply to form the thorax.

8 Holding the hackletip with hackle pliers, wind on three or four evenly spaced turns. Secure the hackletip at the eye and remove the excess. Finally, build a small, neat head and cast off the thread with a whip finish.

See also	RIBBING, PAGE 22
	HAIRWING, PAGE 26

Peeping Caddis

This is a heavily weighted pattern designed to be bumped along the bottom of a river or lake—the caddis larvae's habitat.

Close turns of lead wire are used for the underbody combined with a gold tungsten bead to get the Peeping Caddis down deep as quickly as possible. The body is formed from dubbed hare's fur containing plenty of the stiffer guard hairs, whereas the fly's action comes from a long, mobile hackle of brown partridge. This feather is used in a number of wet fly patterns, but is ideal for larger nymphs and bugs, too. The peeping body is created simply by burning one end of a strand of Sparkle yarn.

RECIPE

HOOK:	*Size 8–12 longshank*
THREAD:	*Olive*
TAIL:	*Cream Sparkle yarn*
RIB:	*Gold wire*
BODY:	*Hare's fur*
HACKLE:	*Brown partridge*
HEAD:	*Gold tungsten bead*

1 Before fixing the hook in the vise, slip on a gold bead then apply a lead wire underbody. Take a short length of cream Sparkle yarn and melt one end so that it forms a dark blob.

FISH FOR:

Brown trout

Grayling

Rainbow trout

2 With the tying thread at the bend of the hook, catch in the Sparkle yarn so that the waste end fits in the gap to the rear of the weighted underbody. This suggests the larva's peeping body.

Cream Sparkle yarn
The yarn suggests the body coming peeping out from the case of a caddis larva. Some caddis larvae are free swimming while others build protective cases from sand or small stones.

Gold wire
Gold wire is used here to hold the dubbed hare's fur in place.

Hare's fur
Natural hare's fur with plenty of the stiff guard hairs mixed with the softer, easier to dub underfur creates a very natural-looking case for a caddis larva without the need to add small stones or bits of twig. It's more effective too.

Brown partridge
The speckled brown fibers of partridge feather can be used to great effect on a variety of soft hackle patterns. Here we use the larger feathers that are typically discarded. With this pattern the longer and more mobile the hackle, the better.

Gold bead
Metal beads come in a number of sizes and colors, with gold the most popular. Use either normal gold beads, or if the water is deep and fast, opt for the ultraheavy tungsten bead.

3 Select a large, well-marked brown partridge body feather. Stroke the fibers against the grain so that the tip is exposed. Catch the feather in by this tip at the base of the yarn tail.

4 Take hold of the partridge feather by the end of its stem and wind on two full turns. Stroke the fibers back past the bend as each turn is applied.

5 Secure the end stem of the hackle with thread, then remove the excess. Catch in 2 inches (5 cm) of gold wire before dubbing on a large pinch of hare's fur to well-waxed tying thread.

6 Wind the dubbed hare's fur toward the gold bead so that it covers the underbody. Apply a reverse taper so that the body gets slightly thinner toward the eye.

7 Take the gold wire and wind it along the body in open, evenly spaced turns. Four or five turns are ample even for a fly of this size.

8 When the wire reaches the bead, secure the loose end and remove the excess. Cast off the tying thread with a whip finish before ragging out some of the hare's fur with a dubbing needle.

See also   DUBBING (SIMPLE), PAGE 28

WEIGHTED UNDERBODY, PAGE 34

Crystal Cat

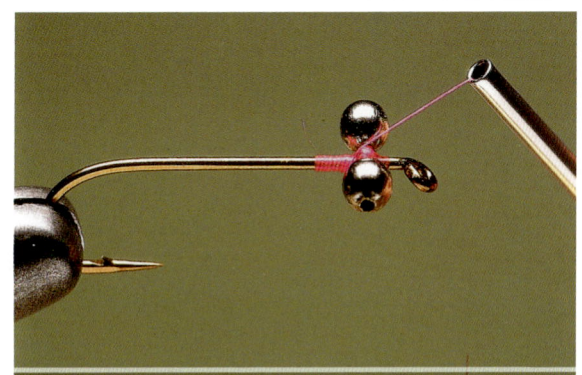

This is an all-coral pink version of the basic Cat's Whisker. The original is tied with a fluorescent chartreuse body of either normal chenille or Crystal Chenille, and has a wing and tail of white marabou. Marabou is a superb material for winging streamers, and imparts a pulsating, swimming action on every pull of the retrieve. Using it for the wing and tail only enhances this effect. The Crystal Cat's profile, plus the way the pattern is weighted along the body and head, means it flutters down gently after casting, an action that proves so enticing that trout will often take it on the drop.

1 Fix the hook in the vise and run on a solid base of thread just behind the eye. Remove a pair of connected metal chain beads and position them at the top of the hook.

FISH FOR:

Brown trout

Rainbow trout

2 Secure the beads with figure-of-eight thread wraps, working the thread tight around the front and back. Add a drop of Superglue to the wraps and allow to cure.

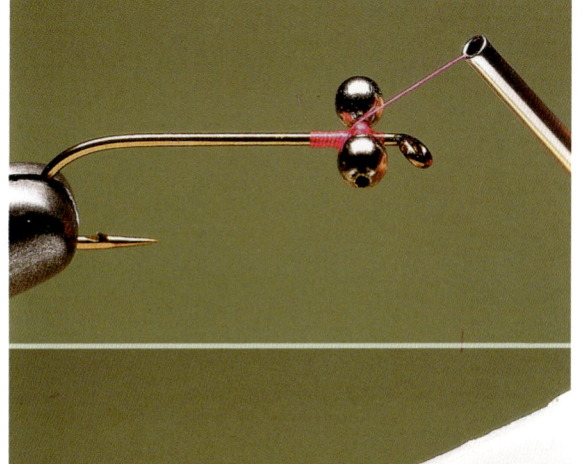

Pink Crystal Chenille

This mylar-based chenille produces a wonderful sparkling body on a wide range of large trout and salmon patterns. Marketed under a range of names including Fritz and Cactus Chenille, it is available in a wide range of colors both dazzling and more subtle.

Pink marabou

This soft, mobile feather, which actually comes from the domestic white turkey, works superbly in a wide range of streamer patterns. It can be used either as a wing, or tail, or both. It imparts wonderful movement to any fly.

Chain beads

These linked metal beads add both weight and sparkle to any streamer pattern. Being lighter than dumbbells, they are best suited to slow-sinking patterns.

Lead wire

This soft but heavyweight wire can be easily wrapped in close turns along the hook to help the fly sink more quickly.

3 Apply close turns of fine lead wire along three-quarters of the remaining hook shank. Leave a small gap at the bend to accommodate the tail before fixing the wire with further thread wraps.

4 Tear off a generous pinch of marabou from the plume. Judge the material for length and trim the butts with scissors. Position the marabou at the bend so the waste ends fill the gap up to the lead-wire underbody.

5 Take 3 inches (7.5 cm) of coral pink Crystal Chenille and strip the material away to expose a short section of the core. Catch the Crystal Chenille in at the tail base by wrapping tying thread over this bare core.

6 Holding the end of the Crystal Chenille wind it along the shank in close turns, stroking the fibers back as each turn is applied. Do not allow any turns to overlap because this will cause an unsightly lump to form.

7 Secure the loose end of the Crystal Chenille at the back of the beads and remove the excess. Next, tear off a second pinch of the pink marabou and catch it in so the tips are level with those of the tail.

8 Secure with tight thread wraps and draw the butts of the marabou between the beads. Apply further tight thread wraps, then trim away the waste ends of marabou. Cast off the thread with a whip finish.

Viva Booby

This big, buoyant eyed fly uses a combination of foam eyes and a marabou tail to make it come alive beneath the water's surface. The foam can be obtained either as a block or in a preformed dowel that is cut to length before the ends are trimmed to create two round eyes.

The Booby is tied in a range of colors from white, orange, or coral pink to plain black, or as here, in black and lime green.

When applying foam eyes use a fairly thick thread that lies flat so it doesn't cut through the soft foam. A drop of Superglue in the thread between the eyes will keep them securely in place. A few very fine pearl strands in the tail may be used to add sparkle.

RECIPE

HOOK:	*Size 8–10 wet fly*
THREAD:	*Black*
EYES:	*Black microcellular foam dowel*
TAG:	*Fluorescent lime green chenille*
TAIL:	*Black marabou and fine pearl strands*
BODY:	*Black chenille*

1 Having fixed the hook in the vise run on close turns of thread just behind the eye. Take a short length of foam dowel and catch it in halfway along its length on top of the hook shank.

FISH FOR:

Brown trout

Rainbow trout

2 Twist the foam so that it now lies across rather than in line with the hook shank. Fix it in this position with tight, figure-of-eight turns of tying thread.

Fine pearl strands

Ultrafine pearl strands such as Mirror Flash add a wonderful sparkle and are so thin and flexible that they don't affect the action of the wing or tail.

Black microcellularfoam

The tiny closed cells of this type of foam make it extremely buoyant— perfect, in fact, for adding buoyancy to either floating flies or those such as the Booby that are fished deep on a fast-sinking line. Microcellular foam is available in a number of forms and for this pattern, block or Booby cord work best.

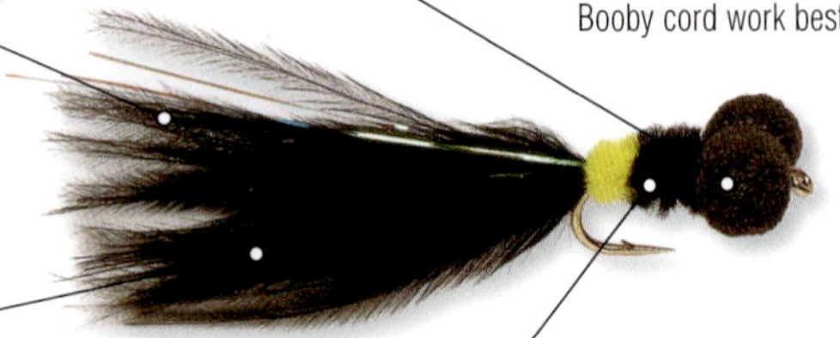

Black marabou

Turkey marabou is a wonderful material for injecting life into a whole range of nymph and streamer patterns. Here it is used as the tail, tied long to give bags of action even when the fly is moved slowly.

Chenille

Chenille is a thick, fluffy material spun onto a core. It comes in a range of diameters and colors, both plain and fluorescent. Being so thick it forms bulk quickly and works well on a wide range of streamer patterns such as the Booby. Here a combination of plain black and fluorescent lime green is used to great effect.

3 Once the foam is fixed securely to the hook, trim the end of the dowel to form two eyes. Using small repeated snips rather than large cuts produces the neatest result.

4 Keep trimming carefully until two round eyes of equal size have been formed. Check from the front when judging the proportions.

5 Once the eyes are the correct size and shape, carry the tying thread down to the hook bend. There, catch in a long tail of black marabou with tight thread wraps. Any stray fibers may simply be pinched off.

6 Catch in two or three fine pearl strands at the same point. These should be just enough to add a little sparkle and should not impede the tail action.

7 Secure the waste ends of both materials with tight thread turns, then catch in a length of lime green chenille, first stripping away the flue to expose a small amount of the core. Wind on two full turns to form a bright tag.

8 Secure the end of the lime green chenille and remove the excess. Catch in a length of black chenille at the front of the tag and wind it up to the foam eyes. Secure the loose end, remove the excess, and cast off the thread.

Ultra Clouser

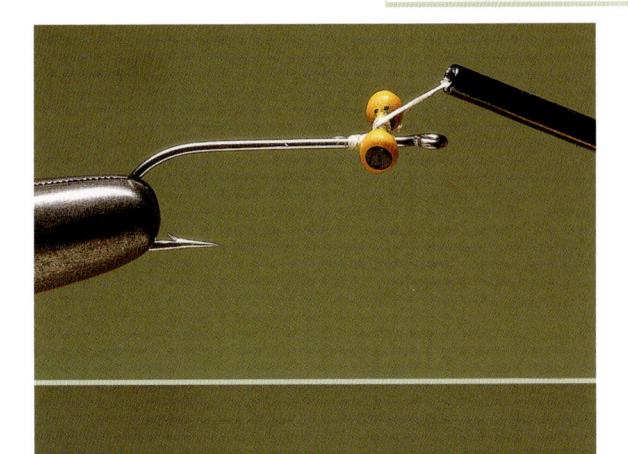

Tough and easy to tie, the original Clouser Minnow is a superb, fast-sinking pattern that works in both fresh- and salt-water. This version is basically the same as the original except that instead of bucktail a man-made product such as Ultra Hair or the finer, more mobile, Slinky is used. Using artificial hair makes the Clouser even more robust, and because artificial hair needs less preparation than bucktail, it is even easier to use.

When tying this pattern always add a longer wing and tail than necessary. These can be trimmed to length in the field, ensuring that you always have a fly of the right size.

RECIPE

HOOK:	*Size 2–8 silvered hook*
THREAD:	*White*
EYES:	*Painted lead dumbbells*
TAIL:	*White Ultra Hair*
WING:	*Chartreuse Ultra Hair and lime Krystal Flash*

1 Fix the hook securely in the vise and run on a solid bed of white tying thread a short distance from the eye. Position a pair of painted dumbbell eyes on top of the shank.

FISH FOR:

Brown trout

Cutthroat

Rainbow trout

2 Secure the eyes in place with tight figure-of-eight thread turns. Apply further turns of thread both in front and behind the eyes to stop them from rotating.

White and chartreuse Ultra Hair

This is a tough man-made fiber that is available in long hanks, making it an ideal material for winging even the largest of flies. It is translucent and mobile, making it ideal for many types of lures, especially those used to represent small fish. The material is available in a wide range of colors.

Krystal Flash

Flash is a very important part of most bait-fish imitations and the Clouser is no exception. A few strands of lime Krystal Flash sandwiched between the wing and body do the job perfectly.

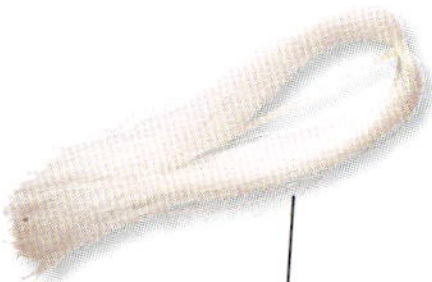

Painted lead dumbbells

When a large amount of weight needs to be added there is little to beat lead dumbbell eyes. These are available in a range of sizes and may be left plain or painted various colors such as yellow, white, and red. Each painted eye is completed by adding a black pupil.

3 Take a 3-inch (7.5-cm)
length of white Ultra Hair
and catch it in place in front of
the eyes with a few tight turns
of thread.

4 Draw the Ultra Hair between
the eyes and secure in
place behind them. Carry the
thread in open turns down to
the bend, fixing the Ultra Hair
securely to the hook shank.

5 Take the thread back up to
the eye of the hook, again
in evenly spaced turns wound
over the Ultra Hair. Invert the
hook in the vise and, at the eye,
catch in a few strands of lime
Krystal Flash.

6 At the same point catch in a 3-inch (7.5-cm)-long bunch of chartreuse Ultra Hair, then secure it in place by adding further tight thread turns.

7 Build a neat head with the tying thread before casting it off with a whip finish. Add a coat of clear lacquer to the bare turns of thread.

8 Return the hook to its original position, then trim the ends of the wing to length creating a slight taper in the process.

See also   HAIRWING, PAGE 26

Tequila Flash

Marabou is a superb material when used in bunches for wings and tails, and for big flies it is also extremely effective when wound as a hackle. The effect is quite incredible, producing a fly that literally pulses with life on every twitch of the retrieve.

The ideal feather for this method is known as a marabou blood, a plume with an even and relatively short fiber length that is just right for tying flies on size 6 hooks and larger.

Any color of marabou works well, though some of the gaudier ones, such as orange, pink, and, purple, work well both for Pacific salmon and Steelhead.

RECIPE

HOOK:	*Size 4–8 black up eyed salmon hook*
THREAD:	*Red*
TAIL:	*Yellow marabou bloods*
BODY:	*Orange fur*
UNDER-WING:	*Gold flashabou and pearl Krystal Flash*
HACKLE:	*Orange marabou bloods*

1 Fix the hook securely in the vise and run the tying thread on at the eye. Wind close turns of thread over the loop eye to secure it firmly.

FISH FOR:

Steelhead

Chinook

Coho

2 Carry the tying thread halfway down the hook shank in touching turns. Select a small, dyed yellow turkey blood feather and stroke the fibers back from the tip before catching it in place.

Gold Flashabou

Fine metallic strands such as Flashabou provide a nice touch of sparkle to any wing or tail. They are also soft and fine enough not to impede the mobility of other wing materials such as marabou. Here gold Flashabou is used to complement the orange and yellow marabou.

Orange and yellow marabou bloods

Marabou is simply the material for tying a vast range of streamer patterns. Its mobility and life when twitched through the water is absolutely superb, providing an action that few predatory fish can resist. Most often used either as a wing or tail, here short-fibered bloods are wound to form a hackle—a method that works extremely well on larger salmon and steelhead patterns.

Krystal Flash

Pearl Krystal Flash adds a fantastic sparkle to any fly. The tiny facets that form in the twisted strands catch the light beautifully on every pulse of the retrieve.

Orange fur

Not strictly necessary to the success of this pattern, orange fur is used here simply to cover the exposed ends of the tail and provide a neat effect.

3 Take the turkey feather by its base and wind on three full turns. Stroke the fibers back at each turn so that they lie back over the hook bend making sure that the turns do not overlap.

4 Secure the loose end of the feather with thread and remove the excess. Stroke the fibers back and position them with turns of tying thread wound around their base.

5 Take a pinch of orange fur and dub it onto the tying thread, then wind the fur in close turns from the base of the tail, stopping a short distance from the eye.

6 Take three or four strands of gold Flashabou. Catch them in at the front of the body, then fold them over to double their number.

7 Do the same with two strands of pearl Krystal Flash, then prepare a dyed orange turkey blood in the same way as for the tail and catch it in by its tip. Wind on three full turns, again stroking the fibers back on each turn.

8 Secure the loose end of the feather at the eye and remove the excess. Stroke the fibers back over the hook and position with further thread turns. Build a neat head and cast off with a whip finish.

| See also | DUBBING (SIMPLE), PAGE 28 |
| | COLLAR HACKLE, PAGE 36 |

Matuka

Originally the name for a species of New Zealand bird whose plumage was first used for this pattern, the term Matuka is now used for this particular style of streamer wing. Tied like a dorsal fin running the length of the fly's body, the wing produces an attractive silhouette and plenty of movement. The main advantage is that the wing cannot wrap around the hook bend like a standard streamer wing so it always swims perfectly.

A body made of chenille, a material that produces a chunky effect, enhances the dense outline. It is a versatile pattern that can suggest anything from small fish to larger invertebrates.

RECIPE

HOOK:	*Size 4–8 longshank*
THREAD:	*Olive*
WEIGHT:	*Medium-diameter lead wire*
RIB:	*Oval gold tinsel*
BODY:	*Olive chenille*
SIDES:	*Lime Krystal Flash*
WING:	*Dyed olive grizzly hackles*
HACKLE:	*Dyed olive grizzly hackles*

1 Fix the hook in the vise and apply an underbody of lead wire. Run the tying thread to the bend and catch in 3 inches (7.5 cm) of oval gold tinsel plus 3 inches (7.5 cm) of olive chenille. Wind the chenille over the turns of lead wire.

FISH FOR:

Brown trout

Cutthroat

Rainbow trout

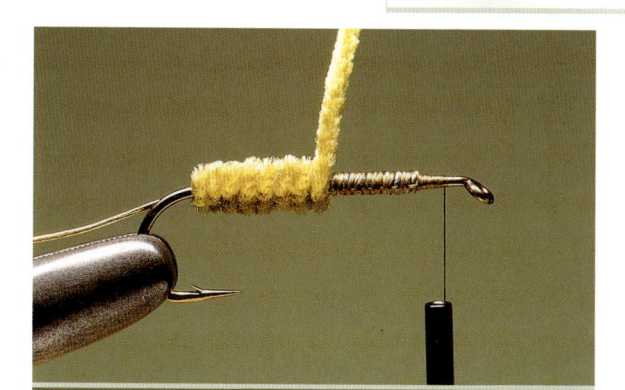

2 Continue winding the chenille so that it covers the length of the underbody. Secure, then remove the loose end before selecting two equal-sized pairs of dyed olive grizzly hackles.

Oval gold tinsel

Metal tinsel is available in a range of diameters, the standard colors being gold and silver. It may be used to create entire bodies but is typically used as a ribbing material.

Krystal Flash

This fine pearl strand comes with a rippled effect that sparkles at every turn of the light and is available in a wide range of colors from plain pearl to orange, lime, and olive. It is a great material for wings and tail.

Dyed grizzly hackles

Grizzlyhackles may be dyed various colors to produce interesting mottled effects. Olive is a particularly good color because it suggests a whole range of aquatic creatures from small fish to dragonfly nymphs.

Lead wire

Close turns of lead wire added before the body materials gives extra weight to a fly and helps it to sink quickly.

Olive chenille

This caterpillar-like material is thick and chunky, producing a dense body quickly and easily. It is available in a vast range of colors.

3 Place the hackles together so that all the tips are level. Next gently tear off the fibers along the bottom edge of the wing leaving enough at the tip to form a tail.

4 Catch in the hackles on top of the hook so that the bare lower section corresponds with the body. Take three long strands of lime Krystal Flash and catch them in so the ends project back along the body.

5 Draw the hackles so they sit right on top of the body, at the same time pulling the Krystal Flash into the same position. Part the hackle fibers positioned at the very end of the body and apply one turn of the tinsel rib.

6 Wind the oval tinsel along the body, parting the hackle fibers before each turn is applied. Moistening the fibers slightly will prevent the gap that has been formed from closing too quickly.

7 Once the turns of rib have locked the wing and Krystal Flash to the body, secure the loose end and remove the excess. Prepare a single hackle the same color as the wing and catch it in at the eye.

8 Take hold of the hackletip with pliers and wind on three or four turns to form a collar. Secure the hackletip and remove the excess. Apply a neat head before casting off with a whip finish and trimming the ends of the Krystal Flash.

See also   WEIGHTED UNDERBODY, PAGE 34

COLLAR HACKLE, PAGE 36

Conehead Bugger

This is a quick-sinking version of the ever-popular Woolly Bugger, a marabou-tailed streamer with a ducking diving action that is deadly for both trout and salmon.

Apart from the pulsing marabou tail, the key to the effectiveness of this fly is a dense silhouette produced by a body of chenille and close hackle turns. When using chenille it is important to remove the fluffy herl from a short section of the core before it is caught in. This is to keep bulk to a minimum and will prevent an unsightly bulge from forming at the tail.

RECIPE

HOOK:	*Size 4–8 longshank*
THREAD:	*Black*
WEIGHT:	*Medium-diameter lead wire*
TAIL:	*Olive marabou and olive Krystal Flash*
RIB:	*Black wire*
BODY:	*Black chenille*
HACKLE:	*Black saddle hackle*
HEAD:	*Gold conehead*

1 Before fixing the hook in the vise, slip the conehead over the point, sliding it along the shank to the eye. Remember to apply its pointed end first. Next, wind on close turns of medium width lead wire.

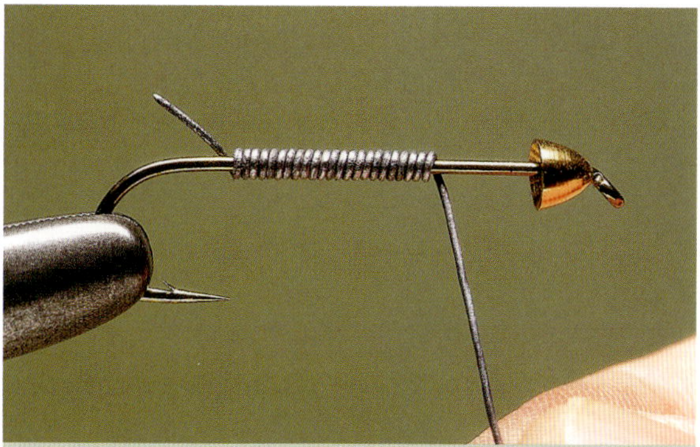

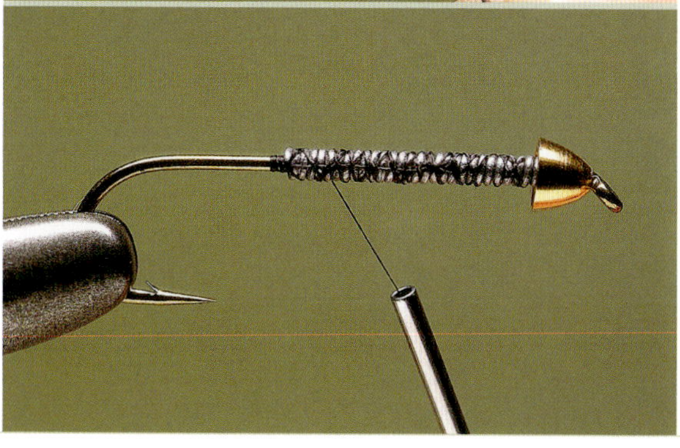

FISH FOR:

Brown trout

Cutthroat

Rainbow trout

2 Push the turns of lead wire along the shank so they fit right into the back of the head, fixing it tight against the hook eye. Leave a gap at the bend for the tail. Secure the wire with tying thread.

Lead wire
Lead wire in various diameters is an ideal material for creating a weighted underbody. It is usually applied to the hook before the other body materials.

Black saddle hackle
When tying body hackles on large patterns, standard cock hackles are often not long enough. Saddle hackles are a better option, being both longer and having a more consistent fiber length.

Black chenille
Thick and chunky chenille is a superb material for the bodies of many large streamer patterns. Being dense it readily adds bulk and can be applied quickly even on big hooks.

Gold conehead
These are a simple development on the standard metal bead. Coneheads are available in a range of sizes and in a variety of colors including gold. They are best suited for adding weight to large streamer patterns.

Olive Krystal Flash
The fine, twisted pearl strands of Krystal Flash catch the light at every turn. They work well when applied to either wings or tails.

Olive marabou
Soft turkey marabou is available in a range of dyed colors including natural ones such as olive. Whatever the color, it always adds life and movement to the fly.

Black wire
Copper wire is now available in a wide range of colors as well as its natural one. Black works well on dark-colored bodies when a very dense feel is required.

3 Tear off a large pinch of olive marabou and catch it in with thread so the waste ends fill the bare shank left between the lead wire and the bend. Also catch in a few strands of olive or pearl Krystal Flash.

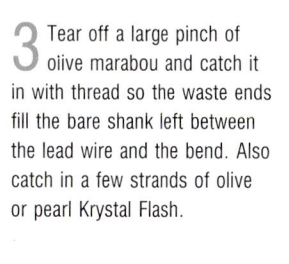

4 Catch in a length of black wire, then wind the thread over the waste ends of the tail materials so that it is the same diameter as the underbody. Remove the flue from a length of black chenille to expose a section of the core.

5 Using tying thread, catch in the chenille at the tail base by this core. Run the tying thread up to the conehead, then follow it with close turns of the chenille.

6 Secure the loose end of the chenille at the rear of the conehead, and remove the excess. Catch in a black saddle hackle that has been prepared by stripping away the downy fibers at its base.

7 Grasp the tip of the hackle with hackle pliers and wind it over the body in open, evenly spaced turns. Continue winding until you reach the tail base.

8 Wind the black wire up through the hackle so that it locks the turns of the hackle's stem in place. Secure the wire and the back of the cone, trim off the excess, and apply a whip finish. Now remove the excess hackletip.

See also   RIBBING SET, PAGE 22

WEIGHTED UNDERBODY, PAGE 34

Minkie

This fly uses fur strip but tied in a similar style to a feather, the Matuka wing being secured along the top of the body with evenly spaced turns of ribbing. The technique produces a very hardy wing that still imparts plenty of movement to the finished fly.

The Minkie is tied as an out-and-out imitation of a small fish with a sparkling body of dubbed Lite Brite ragged out to make the most of its pearly effect.

To form a tight, robust body, rather than simply dubbing the Lite Brite, twist it as it is being wound on the hook.

RECIPE

HOOK:	*Size 4–8 silvered longshank*
THREAD:	*White*
EYES:	*Small stick-on decals*
WEIGHT:	*Lead wire*
TAIL:	*Fluorescent red floss*
RIB:	*Silver wire*
BODY:	*Blue pearl Lite Brite*
WING:	*Gray mink strip*

1 Having secured the hook in the vise, form a weighted underbody from close turns of lead wire. Secure them with tight thread turns before catching in a tail of fluorescent red floss plus 3 inches (7.5 cm) of silver wire at the tail base.

FISH FOR:

Brown trout

Rainbow trout

2 Take a large pinch of Lite Brite and apply it to the thread so it runs to a taper. Dub it on evenly, then make one full turn at the tail. Next, begin to twist the dubbing so that it forms a tight yarn.

Gray mink strip
Finer and shorter than rabbit strip, mink strip is the preferred winging material for this Zonker/Matuka hybrid. When using fur strip in this manner always choose a soft tanned skin so that there is plenty of mobility in the tail.

Silver wire
Along with adding a small amount of sparkle to the body the silver wire rib is a robust way of fixing the mink strip to the top of the body. Medium-width wire is perfect for this job.

Fluorescent red floss
To add a flash of color to this otherwise pale-colored fly fluorescent red floss is used for the tail. Because fluorescent floss is quite thin the strand must be doubled two or three times to achieve the required bulk.

Stick-on decals
This pattern imitates a small fish so eyes are a must. The original called for jungle cock but small stick-on decals are cheaper and, if anything, even more effective.

Lead wire
Lead wire wound in a single or double layer along the hook shank is the preferred method of adding weight to this and other similar patterns. Wound in close turns the wire is concealed under the body materials.

Pearl Lite Brite
Lite Brite is a coarse, manmade dubbing material that is superb for creating a sparkling body. There are three forms of pearl Lite Brite, the two best having a slight blue or green tinge. The material rags out well so that every little fiber catches the light.

3 Continue winding the dubbed Lite Brite along the hook shank. Toward the middle of the hook allow the dubbing to untwist a little so that it forms a slight bulge.

4 Once the Lite Brite has reached a short distance from the eye, take a strip of mink, still on the skin, and catch it in at the eye. The skin should project just past the bend of the hook.

5 Stretch the skin until it sits close along the top of the body. Divide the hair that is positioned at the end of the body and wind on one tight turn of silver wire so that it is in direct contact with the skin.

6 Wind the wire in evenly spaced turns through the hair, securing the skin strip to the body with each turn. Moistening the hair a little will help to keep it out of the way as each turn is applied.

7 Having reached the front of the wing, secure the loose end of the wire and remove the excess plus the waste end of the mink strip. Build a pronounced head, cast off with a whip finish, then rag out the body with Velcro.

8 Apply a small stick-on eye to either side of the head, then apply three or four coats of clear lacquer to fix the eyes in place.

See also   DUBBING (SIMPLE), PAGE 28

WEIGHTED UNDERBODY, PAGE 34

Egg-sucking Leech

RECIPE

HOOK:	*Size 8–4 longshank*
THREAD:	*Black*
WEIGHT:	*Lead wire*
TAIL:	*Black rabbit strip— straightcut*
BODY:	*Black rabbit strip— crosscut*
CHEEKS:	*Pearl Krystal Flash*
HEAD:	*Fluorescent orange chenille*

Using rabbit strip wound along the body is a wonderful way of adding both bulk and action to a big heavy fly such as the Egg-sucking Leech. When creating the body hackle, always use a strip of rabbit cut across the grain of the hair rather than with it as would be used when tying a Zonker wing. Using the crosscut strip allows the fur to lie back over the hook, giving a sleek profile and ensuring that the fly pulses enticingly in the water.

The technique of winding rabbit-strip bodies can be used to tie all types of big mobile patterns, including imitations of types of dragonfly nymphs and even small fish.

1 Fix the hook in the vise and wind on close turns of lead wire along the shank. Overlap the turns of wire at the head to form a double layer, adding extra weight at the head end.

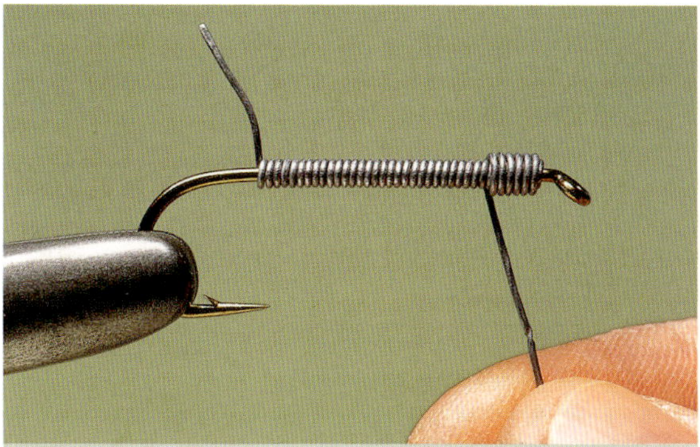

FISH FOR:

Brown trout

Cutthroat

Coho

2 Secure the turns of lead wire with close turns of tying thread. Take the thread down to the bend and there catch in a short length of dyed black rabbit strip.

Black rabbit strip
Rabbit strip is a tough yet mobile material that works well in a large number of streamer patterns. Here it is used cut into thin strips both for the tail and for the action-packed body hackle. This material may be obtained either in patches or precut into thin strips.

Pearl Krystal Flash
Though the original Egg-sucking Leech has a very dark feel to it, adding just a touch or sparkle in the form of a few strands of pearl Krystal Flash can make it even more effective.

Lead wire
Lead wire is the perfect material for adding weight to all but the smallest patterns. Wound in close turns along the hook shank, it is concealed beneath any body materials.

Fluorescent orange chenille
The orange head of this pattern contrasts beautifully with the black hue of the body and tail. Fluorescent orange chenille is ideal for this purpose as it is tough and adds just the right amount of bulk.

3 Take another, longer length of rabbit strip, this time cut across the direction in which the hair lies rather than in line with it. Catch this in at the base of the tail.

4 Wind the thread up the shank to the rear of the head. Next, wind the rabbit strip over the lead wire underbody in close but not overlapping turns. Stroke the hairs back after each wrap.

5 Continue winding the strip until it has reached the base of the head. Secure the loose end with thread and remove the excess. At this point the turns of hair should all sweep back toward the tail.

6 Take three strands of pearl Krystal Flash and catch them in halfway along their length immediately in front of the body. Fold them over so they are positioned along either side of the body.

7 Take a length of fluorescent orange floss and strip away a short section of the flue to expose the core. Catch in the chenille by this bare core section just in front of the body.

8 Take the thread up to the eye, following it with close turns of the chenille to form a pronounced head. Secure the loose end of the chenille and remove the excess, then cast off the thread with a whip finish.

See also WEIGHTED UNDERBODY, PAGE 34

Black Stonefly Nymph

This pattern imitates the nymph of any of the large, dark species of Stonefly. To obtain the same flattened profile as the real nymph, a length of square lead is run along either side of the main underbody. This has the advantage of adding even more weight to the fly, helping it to sink quickly in fast-flowing water.

The all-important wing cases are formed from slips of dark turkey tail with a V-shaped cut made in one end. To prevent the turkey tail from splitting, it is reinforced by flexible cement applied to the back of the feather before use.

RECIPE

HOOK:	*Size 4–10 USD Nymph hook*
THREAD:	*Black*
WEIGHT:	*Square lead wire*
TAIL:	*Black goose biots*
RIB:	*Black Magic Glass*
BODY:	*Dyed black rabbit fur*
WING CASES:	*Black turkey tail*
LEGS:	*Rubber strands*

1 Fix the hook in the vise and wind on close turns of square lead wire. Secure with thread, then take a second length and position it around the sides of the underbody. This creates a more flattened profile.

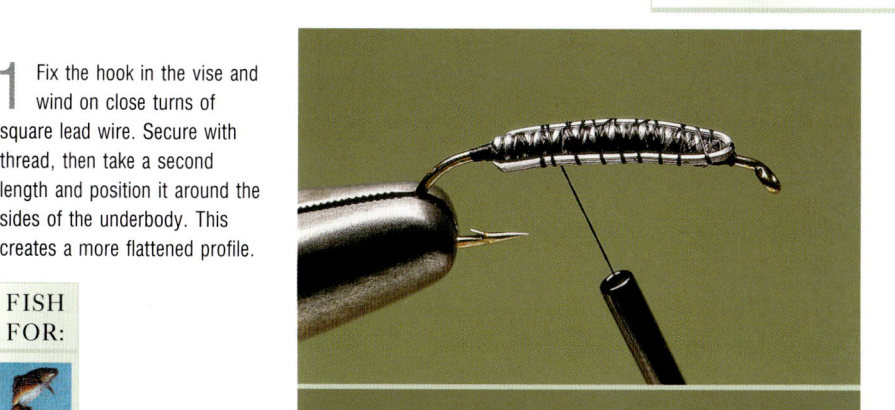

FISH FOR:

Brown trout

Rainbow trout

Cutthroat

2 Secure the lead wire with tight thread turns taking the thread to a position opposite the barb of the hook. There, catch in two dyed black goose biots, one on either side of the shank.

Dyed black rabbit fur

Rabbit fur is a great natural dubbing as it is cheap and available in a wide range of dyed colors. Ensuring that plenty of the stiffer guard hairs are used with the soft underfur creates a wonderful "buggy" effect.

Black turkey tail

This material is used for the wing cases of the Stonefly nymph. It is quite tough but, even so, needs to be reinforced with a coat of flexible cement on its back to stop it from splitting.

Black Nymph Glass

Plastic strands such as Magic Glass and Swannundaze are tough, flexible, and translucent, making them brilliant ribbing materials for big nymphs and also for some streamer bodies. They have a D-shaped profile and are available in a wide range of colors.

Black goose biots

Goose biots are the short spiky fibers found on the bad side of a goose primary feather. They make great tails and antennae on Stonefly Nymphs.

Square lead wire

An angled profile means that square lead works better for shaped underbodies than the round version because the edges stop it from slipping so easily.

Black rubber strands

Rubber strands of all kinds add a real kick to any pattern, whether a dry fly, streamer, or nymph. Here, black ones are used to match the body color.

3 At the same point catch in 3 inches (7.5 cm) of black Magic Glass, securing it firmly in the gap between the lead underbody and the tail. Dub on a large pinch of dyed black rabbit fur and wind it over the underbody in close turns.

4 Carry the dubbed fur up toward the eye, stopping at the point where the hook shank is bent. Take hold of the Magic Glass and stretch it slightly before winding on in open, evenly spaced turns.

5 When the rib has been wound the full length of the body, secure the loose end and remove the excess. Next, take a strip of dark turkey tail and cut a V-shaped notch in one end.

6 Position the strip of turkey tail with tying thread so that it sits low over the forward end of the body. Remove any excess feather, then cover the butts with a pinch of dubbed black rabbit fur.

7 Take a second strip of dark turkey tail and prepare and apply as before. That done, catch in two black rubber strands, one on either side of the thorax so they form four legs.

8 Apply a short section of dubbed rabbit fur followed by a third set of turkey tail wing cases. Catch in two dyed black goose biots as antennae before applying a pinch of dubbed black rabbit fur to complete the thorax.

See also   DUBBING (SIMPLE), PAGE 28

WEIGHTED UNDERBODY, PAGE 34

Blue Charm

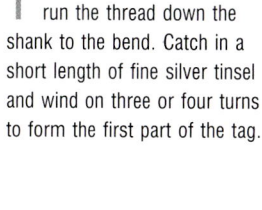

The Blue Charm is a classic but simply tied Atlantic salmon pattern. Originally, the wing was tied from brown mallard overlaid with thin strips of teal or pintail. Today, however, to make it more robust and even simpler, it is normally tied in this hairwinged version using gray squirrel tail.

When applying a floss body, especially when using the thicker rayon types, counterwind the floss because this will allow the fibers to spread and lie flat. This helps give a nice smooth body.

When applying the hackle, a little trick known as "doubling" helps the fibers to lie so they sweep back close to the body.

RECIPE

HOOK:	*Size 4–10 salmon single or double*
THREAD:	*Black*
TAG:	*Oval silver tinsel and yellow floss*
TAIL:	*Golden pheasant topping*
RIB:	*Oval silver tinsel*
BODY:	*Black floss*
WING:	*Squirrel tail*
HACKLE:	*Dyed blue cock hackle*

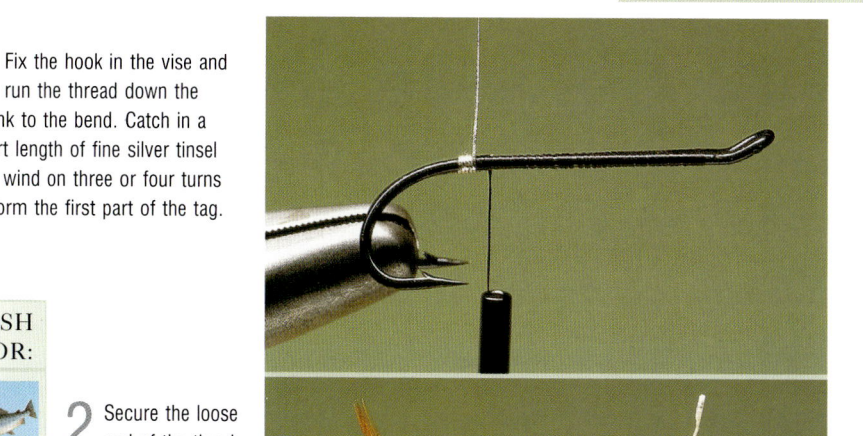

1 Fix the hook in the vise and run the thread down the shank to the bend. Catch in a short length of fine silver tinsel and wind on three or four turns to form the first part of the tag.

FISH FOR:

Atlantic Salmon

2 Secure the loose end of the tinsel, then catch in a length of yellow floss. Wind it to form the second part of the tag. At the front of the tag catch in 3 inches (7.5 cm) of oval silver tinsel plus a golden pheasant topping.

Golden pheasant topping
The sparkling golden crest feathers of the golden pheasant are used for the tail in many salmon patterns.

Yellow floss
The tag on a salmon fly is normally made up of two parts: metal tinsel and floss. Yellow floss is one of the most common colors used and may be either traditional silk or man-made rayon.

Gray squirrel tail
The hair from the gray squirrel is both fine and strong with a gray and brown mottling tipped with white. Here, it is used plain but the hair can also be dyed a wide range of colors for use in other patterns.

Fine oval silver tinsel
This type of metal tinsel comes in a variety of diameters and colors. Of the colors available, the two most commonly used are gold and silver. The latter is used as part of the tag for many Atlantic salmon flies.

Medium oval silver tinsel
On most large flies such as those used to catch salmon, a medium-width tinsel looks in proportion and also adds a nice sparkle to the body.

Black floss
Floss gives the smooth effect required for the body of flies such as the Blue Charm. Natural silk may be used but man-made rayon lasts longer and has even more shine.

Dyed blue cock hackle
For large wet flies such as those used for salmon, dyed cock hackles are the most often used. These should be a nice clear color (here it is blue) with soft, slightly webby fibers that add more life than stiffer types. Both neck and saddle hackles work equally well.

3 Cover the waste ends of the materials with close turns to form an even base for the body. Snip away any excess before catching in a length of black floss. Wind the floss in close turns down to the tail.

4 Once the floss has reached the tail, wind it back up the shank to its catching-in point. Overlapping the floss slightly will help create a slight taper. Secure the loose end of floss and wind on five open, evenly spaced turns of tinsel.

5 Secure the loose end of the tinsel and remove the excess. Next, catch in a dyed blue hackle at the eye, stroking back the fibers so they all lie on one side of the stem. This process is known as doubling.

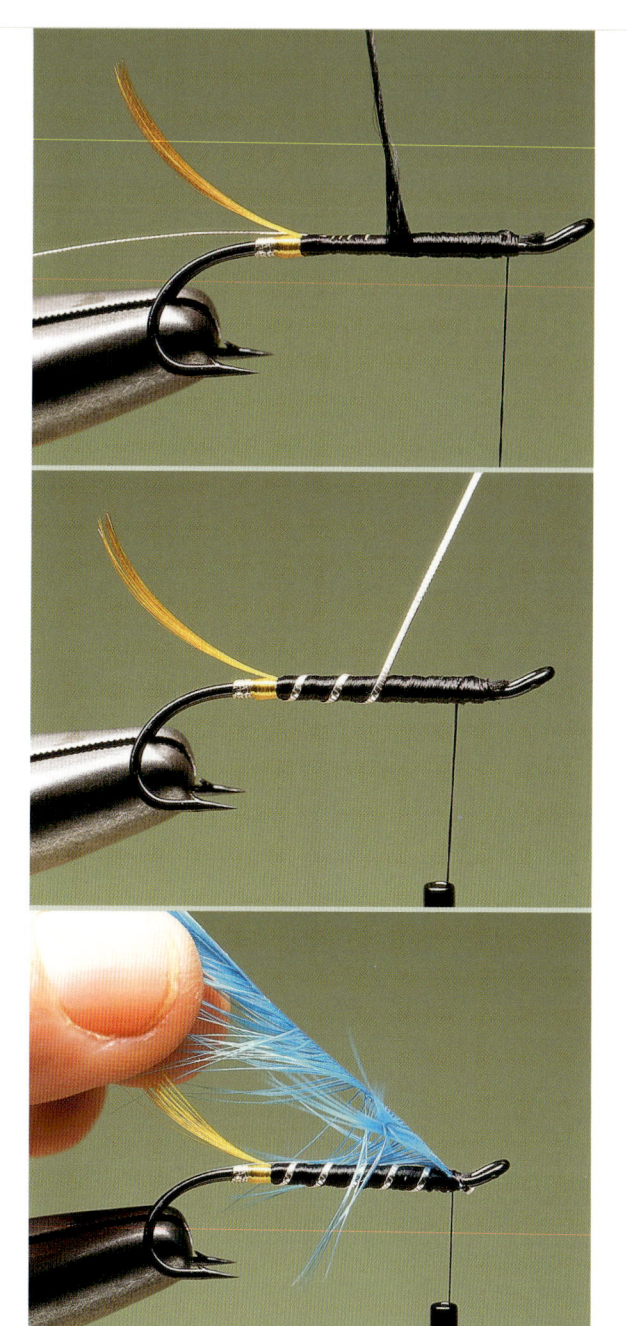

6 Using hackle pliers, wind on three full turns of the hackle so that the fibers sweep back over the body. Work toward the eye, remembering not to let the turns overlap. Secure the loose end of hackle and remove the excess.

7 Stroke the hackle fibers beneath and to the sides of the body. Position them with turns of thread. Take a bunch of gray squirrel tail and trim the butts so it fills the space between the eye and the tail. Position with thread turns.

8 Apply a locking turn of thread around the wing base, then add further tight thread turns around the hair to secure it firmly in place. Build a neat head and cast off with a whip finish, then add a couple of coats of lacquer.

See also	HAIRWING, PAGE 26
	FLOSS BODY, PAGE 44

Rabbit Sculpin

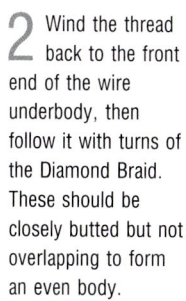

This pattern imitates a small, bottom-dwelling fish known as the Sculpin or Bullhead. The natural is a mottled brown color with a large head and a tapered body, which suits this Zonker-winged pattern perfectly.

Zonker wings are formed from a strip of rabbit fur still on the skin, a technique that makes them very robust. It also means that the wing can be tied long enough to impart plenty of movement. Due to the tapered profile of the Zonker wing, this is a particularly good method for tying a range of fish imitations including the Sculpin. Eyes may be added and are attached by first working a small amount of epoxy into either side of the head.

RECIPE

HOOK:	*Size 2–6 longshank*
THREAD:	*White*
EYES:	*Stick-on decals (optional)*
WEIGHT:	*Lead wire*
BODY:	*Pearl Diamond Braid*
WING:	*Natural gray rabbit*
OVER-WING:	*Tan marabou or chickabou*
HEAD:	*Dyed brown and white deer hair*

1 Fix the hook in the vise and apply close turns of lead wire along the hook shank. Secure them with close turns of thread before catching in a length of pearl Diamond Braid at the bend.

FISH FOR:

Brown trout

Cutthroat

Rainbow trout

2 Wind the thread back to the front end of the wire underbody, then follow it with turns of the Diamond Braid. These should be closely butted but not overlapping to form an even body.

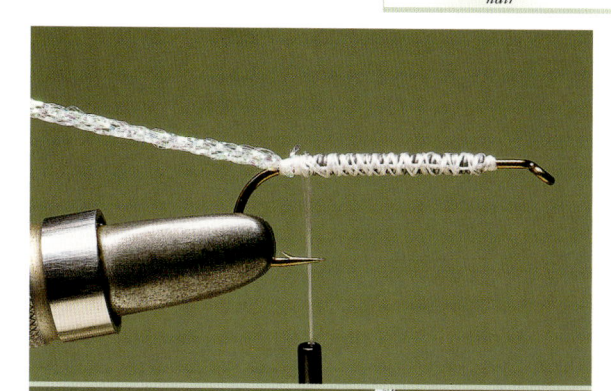

Natural gray rabbit
Rabbit fur is a great material for a wide range of fly-tying uses. Here the tanned skin is cut into thin strips to form the wing of the Sculpin. This method of using rabbit strips works well on a wide range of patterns from fish imitations to leeches.

Pearl Diamond Braid
This woven material is available in a range of metallic colors including gold, silver, and pearl. Being quite thick it builds bulk quickly while the multifaceted texture gives plenty of sparkle.

White and dyed brown deer hair
Dyed brown deer hair is simply white or plain gray deer hair dyed brown and is a way of producing a fly that more closely matches the color of a real Sculpin.

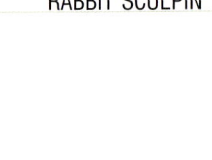
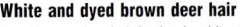

Tan marabou or Chickabou
To widen the front end of this fly and make the profile more like that of a Sculpin, an overwing of marabou may be added to the Zonker wing. This can be either of dyed tan Chickabou, which is the downy base of large grizzly hackles, or plain tan marabou colored with a marker pen.

Lead wire
For bait-fish patterns designed to fish close to the lake or riverbed, lead wire is an ideal way of adding weight.

Stick-on decal eyes
Eyes are a very important trigger point when it comes to tying imitations of small fish. On this pattern the eyes used are larger than those of a real Sculpin, acting, hopefully, as a superstimulus.

3 Take a thin strip of rabbit fur, still on the skin, and catch it in so that its tail end projects just past the bend. Secure the strip in place with tight turns of thread, then cast off with a whip finish.

4 Run the thread back on the bend, then stretch the rabbit strip over the top of the body and secure with tight thread turns. The hair should be divided at this point to ensure that the thread is in direct contact with the actual skin.

5 Cast off the thread with a whip finish and run it back on at the front of the wing. There, catch in a pinch of tan chickabou or plain marabou, which is then given a mottled appearance by applying dabs of color with a marker pen.

6 Next, take a big pinch of dyed brown deer hair and secure it just in front of the wing. Do not allow it to spin but instead, secure it in place on the upper side of the hook.

7 Invert the hook in the vise and apply a similar-sized bunch of white deer hair, again ensuring that it doesn't rotate but remains in a defined layer. Secure with tight thread turns worked through the hair.

8 Return the hook to its original position, then cast off the thread with a whip finish. Trim the head so that it is flat underneath and rounded on top to suggest the shape of the natural Sculpin.

See also   SPINNING DEER HAIR, PAGE 38

WEIGHTED UNDERBODY, PAGE 34

Polar Fry

This fly is tied with a soft, man-made fiber that is basically teddy bear fur. Its fine texture and mobility make it a great material for tying small hairwing patterns and bait-fish imitations, especially when it is used in layers to build the profile of a small fish.

The epoxy head makes the Polar Fry extremely tough as well as adding a small amount of weight and securing those all-important eyes in place.

When using epoxy resin, always use a fast-curing type such as five-minute Devcon, which is also very clear and lets the materials beneath shine through.

RECIPE

HOOK:	*Size 4–10 short-shank carp hook*
THREAD:	*White GP thread*
EYES:	*Stick-on decals*
WING:	*White, olive, and gray Polar Fiber plus strands of silver Flashabou*
GILLS:	*Fluorescent orange floss*
HEAD:	*Clear five-minute epoxy such as Devcon*

1 Fix the hook in the vise and run on a few turns of thread immediately behind the eye. Snip off a bunch of white Polar Fibers from its patch and catch them in with two or three thread turns.

FISH FOR:

Brown trout

Rainbow trout

2 Take a couple of strands of silver Flashabou and catch in halfway along their length before folding them over to form four strands. Position with a couple of thread turns.

Flashabou

Fine, metallic, plastic strands are perfect for adding flash to the wing of many streamer and bait-fish patterns. Being soft and tarnish-free they keep their sparkle indefinitely and don't detract from the mobility of the other wing or tail materials.

Polar Fiber

This is a fine, soft manmade fiber that is perhaps better known as teddy bear fur. It is relatively short but still works well on patterns up to approximately 2 inches (5 cm) making it perfect for small bait-fish and saltwater patterns. It is available in a wide range of colors and may be used singly or in combination.

Fluorescent orange floss

Fluorescent materials have a long and well-deserved reputation for adding vibrancy to any fly pattern. Here a couple of strands of floss are used to suggest the flush of color in the fish's gills.

Stick-on decals

All imitations of small fish benefit from the addition of eyes as these form a major trigger point for predatory fish such as trout. Simple stick-on decals are the easiest and cheapest solution and are available in a range of sizes, colors, and finishes. They are also very light and are perfect for patterns designed to fish near the surface.

3 Remove a bunch of olive
Polar Fiber from its patch,
making sure that it is of the
same density and length as the
white. Catch it in so its tips are
level with those of the white
Polar Fiber.

4 Repeat the procedure with
a slimmer bunch of gray
Polar Fiber, catching it in on
top of the olive. Next, invert
the hook in the vise and catch
in a strand of fluorescent
orange floss, doubling it over
to make two.

5 Carefully mix some clear,
two-part epoxy, keeping
the amount small so the
number of air bubbles is kept
to a minimum. Apply a touch
to where the floss strands are
positioned so they stick close
to the wing.

6 Return the hook to its original position and apply the remainder of the epoxy, working it evenly around the front of the wing. Remove from the vise and rotate for a couple of minutes until the epoxy begins to cure.

7 With the base of the head now formed, add a stick-on eye to either side before the epoxy has fully cured.

8 Finally, mix and apply a second coat of epoxy so that the eyes are fixed in place and the head has the correct bulk. Keep gently rotating the fly so the epoxy is evenly distributed while it hardens.

See also HAIRWING, PAGE 26

Deer Hair Fry

This is a superbly effective pattern when fish are feeding on small dead and dying bait fish hanging just under the surface. It may be tied in the standard profile or side on so that it floats on its side like the real thing.

The Deer Hair Fry is basically a giant Muddler head trimmed into the shape of a small fish. Apply the same principles as for spinning bunches of deer hair, then compact them to form an even consistency and shape them with scissors or a scalpel blade.

To make the pattern more lifelike it should be colored on its upper side with waterproof marker pens. The prominent eyes are a major trigger point in fry imitations.

RECIPE

HOOK:	*Size 2–6 silvered longshank*
THREAD:	*White ultrastrong*
EYES:	*Stick-on decals*
TAIL:	*Gray marabou and pearl Krystal Flash*
BODY:	*White deer hair colored with waterproof marker pens*
PECTORAL FINS:	*Pearl Krystal Flash*

1 Having fixed the hook in the vise, run on close turns of thread along the entire length of the hook shank to provide a solid base for the body. At the bend catch in a pinch of gray marabou plus a few strands of Krystal Flash.

FISH FOR:

Brown trout

2 Take a pinch of white deer hair and offer it up to the hook so that the tips project over the tail. Wind on two or three loose turns of thread, then begin to pull the thread tight. This will cause the hair to flare around the hook.

Rainbow trout

White deer hair
Plain white deer hair works best for
this type of pattern because not only
does it keep the fly floating in the
water's surface, but it can also be
readily colored with waterproof
marker pens. This method of
spinning the hair, then cutting it
to shape is the same as for other
types of deer hair.

Stick-on decals
Eyes are an important trigger
point for many predatory fish
so it is important to incorporate
them in any bait fish imitation.
For patterns such as the Deer
Hair Fry, stick-on decals are
both light and cheap and are
available in a range of sizes
and colors.

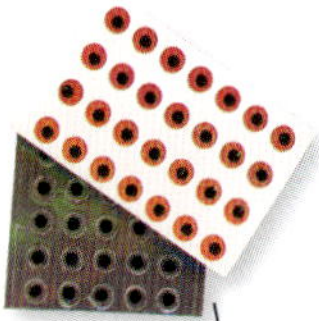

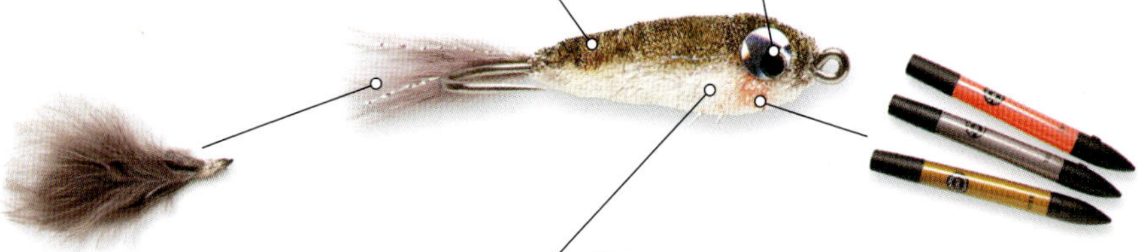

Gray marabou
Marabou is always a good
material to work with when
movement is required from a fly.
This is especially important with
patterns such as the Deer Hair
Fry that are fished almost static.

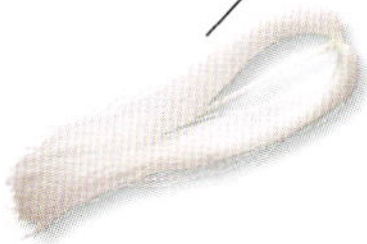

Pearl Krystal Flash
The tiny facets in a strand of
Krystal Flash catch the light
superbly making it a great
material for adding sparkling
fins to any bait fish imitation.

Waterproof marker pens
These are available in a vast
range of colors and may be used
either to add marking to large
nymphs or, as here, to add color
to mimic the countershading of
a small fish. After applying
colors to the hair they should be
blended together by rubbing with
a piece of tissue paper.

3 Once this first bunch of hair has been applied evenly, wind further tight thread turns through the fibers, then draw the hair back and fix in position by winding more thread turns in front.

4 Repeat the process two or three more times until three-quarters of the hook has been covered. Use similar amounts of hair each time to keep the density consistent.

5 Catch in a few strands of pearl Krystal Flash in front of the deer hair. Keep the ends long so that the deer hair can be trimmed without accidentally cutting off the Krystal Flash in the process.

6 Add a further bunch of hair so that the hook is covered right up to the eye. Draw the hair back from the eye and apply a few more tight turns, then cast off the thread with a whip finish.

7 Using sharp, fine-pointed scissors, begin to shape the body. Use small controlled snips to get the basic profile, only making larger cuts to flatten the sides.

8 Color the upper side of the body to mimic the countershading of a small fish using gray and olive pens plus a touch of pink to suggest the gills. Finally, use clear epoxy to stick a decal eye to the underside.

See also   SPINNING DEER HAIR, PAGE 38

Dave's Hopper

During the height of summer when big, colorful grasshoppers are around, this pattern is the best imitation you can use. It has all the recognition points needed to fool big, hopper-feeding trout; the only difference between this and the Dave Whitlock original is that the yarn body has been substituted by one of foam, making it even more buoyant. Remember though, to use thread that lies flat; otherwise, it will slice through the foam when pulled tight.

The toughest part of this pattern is making the legs, which are constructed from dyed yellow grizzly hackles knotted and bent after first trimming the fibers short.

RECIPE

HOOK:	*Size 6–12 longshank*
THREAD:	*Brown*
TAIL:	*Red deer hair*
BODY:	*Yellow foam dowel*
WING:	*Oak turkey quill*
HACKLE:	*Brown cock saddle hackle*
LEGS:	*Dyed yellow grizzly hackles*
HEAD:	*Natural deer hair*

1 Having secured the hook in the vice, run the thread down to the bend. Catch in a pinch of red deer hair as a tail. Use tight, then soft controlling turns to prevent flaring. Cut one end of the foam dowel to a point.

FISH FOR:

Brown trout

Cutthroat

Rainbow trout

2 Catch the foam post in at the bend so the point partly covers the tail. If the foam has a firm texture, it will be necessary to cut a slit in the underside to allow the hook shank to bed into it.

Red deer hair
Dyed red deer hair imitates the red flash to the rear of some brightly colored hoppers. It also adds a little extra buoyancy.

Oak turkey quill
Oak turkey quills have a wonderful mottled appearance that makes them ideal for forming wings on both hopper and caddis-fly patterns. They can be expensive and difficult to obtain but acceptable substitutes are available.

Brown cock saddle hackle
For large patterns saddle hackles have a number of advantages over neck hackles. Their fiber length is more even and, more important, they are long enough to cover the full length of a long hook shank.

Dyed yellow grizzly hackles
Being so tough and flexible, hackles make brilliant legs for both Hopper and cricket imitations. The best method is to stroke all the fibers back so that they sit at right angles to the stem before trimming them short with sharp scissors.

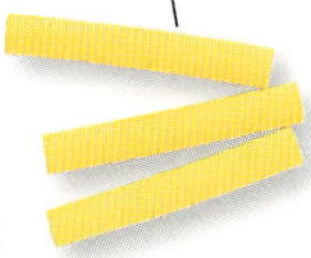

Yellow foam dowel
Foam dowel is an ideal material for the body of big, buoyant patterns such as Dave's Hopper. There are various types available, but one of the easiest to obtain is foam posts, which are available in a range of colors. Choose a medium width for a pattern of this size.

Natural deer hair.
Deer hair not only adds buoyancy and bulk to a fly but can also be easily trimmed into a variety of shapes. Here it is used to imitate the bulky head of a grasshopper and so should be quite high and flat at the front rather than teardrop-shaped, as is the case with a standard muddler head.

3 Select a short-fibered brown cock saddle hackle. Prepare it and catch it in with a couple of thread turns at the same point that the foam was caught in.

4 Wind the thread down over the foam in open turns. Use tight multiple turns at each segment to secure the foam to the hook. That done, wind the hackle in the grooves made by the thread.

5 Secure the hackle tip and remove the waste end. Next, trim the hackle fibers on top of the body to allow the wing to sit low. The wing comprises a rolled slip of oak turkey quill that has been reinforced with a flexible adhesive.

6 Secure the wing, then add a couple of softer turns to make it sit low. Next, take two dyed yellow grizzly hackles and trim the fibers short. Knot each strand to create a leg joint and catch one in either side of the wing.

7 Take a large pinch of natural deer hair and catch it in so the mottled brown tips project over the wing. Pull the thread tight so that the hair flares around the hook shank.

8 Add further bunches of hair until the gap between wing and eye is filled. Cast off the thread with a whip finish before trimming what is basically a muddler head to shape. Keep it high on top like a real hopper's head.

See also   SPINNING DEER HAIR, PAGE 38

Suppliers

NORTH AMERICA

Badger Creek Fly Tying
622 West Dryden Road
Freeville, NY 13068
Tel: (607) 347 4946
www.mwflytying.com

The Bearlodge Angler
612 Grace Avenue
Worland, WY 82401
Tel: (307) 347 4002
Fax: (307) 347 3371
www.w3trib.com/-kmorris

Dan Bailey's Fly Shop
209 West Park Street
PO Box 1019
Livingston, MT 59047
Tel: (406) 222 1673
Fax: (406) 222 8450
www.dan-bailey.com

FishUSA.com
2315 West Grandview Blvd.
Erie, PA 16506
Tel: (814) 835 3600
Fax: (814) 835 3671
www.fishusa.com

Knoll's Yellowstone Hackle
104 Chicory (Fishing Access)
Road
Pray, MT 59065
Tel: (406) 333 4848
www.avicom.net/knoll

Lowe Fly Shop
15 Woodland Drive
Waynesville, NC 28786
Tel: (828) 452 0039
www.loweflyshop.com

North American Angler
211 Moore Dr
Hanover, PA 17331
Tel: (888) 420 0404
www.northamericanangler.com

The Orvis Company
1711 Blue Hills Drive
Roanoke, VA 24012
Tel: (540) 345 4606
Fax: (540) 343 7053
www.orvis.com

Kaufmann's Streamborn Inc
88861 S.W. Commercial
Tigard, Oregon 97223
Tel (503) 639-6400
www.kman.com

Round Rocks Fly Fishing
PO Box 4059
Logan, UT 84323
Tel: (800) 992-8774
www.roundrocks.com

Rocky Mountain Flies
PO Box 76114
Edmonton, Alberta
Canada T6H 5Y7
Tel/Fax: (780) 439 6453
www.rockymountainflies.com

UNI Products J.G. Côté Inc
561 Principale
Ste-Mélanie, QC
Canada J0K 3A0
Tel: (450) 889 2195
Fax: (450) 889 8506
www.uniproducts.com

UK

Ellis Slater
47 Bridge Cross Road
Chase Terrace
Burntwood WS7 8BU
Tel: (01543) 671377

Lyttle's of Dunchurch
2 Southam Road
Dunchurch
Warwickshire CV22 6NL
Tel: (01788) 817044

Farlows
9 Pall Mall
London SW1Y 5LX
Tel: (020) 7839 2423
Fax: (020) 7839 8959
www.farlows.co.uk

Sportfish
Winforton
Hereford HR3 6EB
Tel: (01544) 327 111
Fax: (01544) 327 093
www.sportfish.co.uk

Yorkshire Game Angling
1 Oldgate Lane
Rotherham
South Yorkshire S65 4JX
Tel: 01709 854144
www.yga.yorks.com

Lathkill Limited
19a King Cross Street
Halifax
West Yorkshire HX1 2SH
Tel: 01422 354444
Fax: 01422 350 101
www.lathkill.com

Lakeland Flytying
9 Devonshire Street
Dalton-in-Furnace
Cumbria LA15 8SW
Tel: 01229 465753
www.lakelandflytying.com

Tightlines
Tightlines Direct
72/74 Wind Street
Ammanford
Carmarthenshire SA18 3DR
Tel: 0870 8000123
www.tightlines.co.uk

Glasgow Angling Centre
6 Claythorn Street
Glasgow G40 2HP
Tel: 0141 552 4737

AUSTRALIA AND NEW ZEALAND

The Flyshop
RMB 1270 Goulburn Valley Hwy
Thornton
Vic. 3712, Australia
Tel: (1800) 458 111
Fax: (03) 5773 2514
www.theflyshop.com.au

Flyworld
Anglers International
PO Box 167
Bayswater
WA 6933, Australia
Tel: (08) 9375 8228
www.flyworld.com.au

Pro Tackle
284 Ross River Rd
Townsville
NQ 4814, Australia
Tel: (07) 4775 7677
Fax: (07) 4728 7525
www.protackle.com.au

BCS Enterprises Ltd
PO Box 30361
Lower Hutt
New Zealand
Tel: (64) 4589 3302
www.bcsent.co.nz

Tackle Tactics
PO Box 53
Foxton
New Zealand
Tel: 06 363 5957
Fax: 06 363 5958
www.tackletactics.co.nz

Glossary

Biots

Short, spiky fibers found on the leading edge of a bird's primary wing feather. Used for tails and antennae in stonefly nymph imitations and other general nymph patterns.

Buzzer

Anglers' term for the **Chironomid** midge, usually referring to either the pupa or adult. The name comes from the buzzing noise made by the adults during their mating swarms.

Chironomid

The term for a non-biting midge that is found on both lakes and rivers. Trout feed heavily on the adults, but especially on the aquatic larvae and pupae.

Dry fly

Tied to float on the water's surface, dry flies are available in a wide range of sizes, colors, and forms. Some are tied specifically to imitate a type of aquatic or terrestrial insect while others simply suggest something alive and edible.

Dun

The immature, winged stage of the mayfly. Wings are normally opaque and the tails short. This stage is also known as the **subimago**.

Emerger

General term used to describe an aquatic insect at the point of transforming from the nymph or pupa to the adult.

Hackle

A feather used to represent the legs of a nymph or winged insect. These normally are taken from domestic fowl, either cock or hen, but feathers from game birds such as the partridge, mallard, or grouse are also widely used.

Hair wing

These are large flies tied with a wing comprising various types of hair. They are also known as bucktails because many are tied using the tail hair of the American white-tailed deer.

Imago

The sexually mature stage of the mayfly. The imago is also known as the **spinner**.

Mayfly

The term for the group of insects belonging to the order Ephemeroptera. They can be recognized by their upright, sail-like wings.

Muddler

The term used for the method of creating a bulbous, buoyant head on a fly by spinning and clipping deer body hair.

Nymphs and bugs

The group of artificial flies designed to imitate or simply suggest various types of aquatic invertebrates. These range from small crustaceans to the larvae, pupae, and nymphs of aquatic insects such as the caddis and **mayfly**.

Palmering

The technique of winding a hackle along all or part of a fly's body.

Parachute hackle

A hackle wound around a fly's wing, rather than the hook shank.

Ribbing

A material used to add either sparkle or strength to a fly's body. Types of ribbing materials include flat and oval tinsel, wire, plastic strands, and nylon monofilament.

Seal's fur

A coarse, translucent material used for dubbed bodies in many traditional wet flies. Effective substitutes are now widely available and include products such as **SLF Finesse**, STS Trilobal, and Antron.

SLF Finesse

A translucent dubbing with a fine texture. Available in a wide variety of colors, it is easily blended.

Spent

An insect lying dead on the water's surface. Usually refers to the female of the various **mayfly** species but can also include caddis flies and **Chironomids**.

Spinner

The adult stage of the mayfly. It is normally recognized by its long tail and clear, sparkling wings. The spinner is also known as the **imago**.

Streamer

Streamers are large flies tied with wings made of some type of feather, such as cock hackles or marabou.

Subimago

The immature, winged stage of the mayfly. The subimago is known to anglers as the **dun**.

Terrestrial

An insect or other small invertebrate of non-aquatic origin. This includes grasshoppers, crickets, crane flies, spiders, and some beetles.

Tying thread

Thread of varying colors and diameters that binds the materials used to tie a fly to the hook.

Wing cases

The term used to describe the wing buds of a nymph or pupa. These will be inflated to full size when transformation into the adult insect occurs.

Wet fly

Subsurface patterns tied either to suggest various forms of aquatic insect, or simply to arouse the fish's curiosity.

Index

CREDITS

All photographs and illustrations are the copyright of
Quarto Publishing plc. While every effort has been made
to credit contributors, Quarto would like to apologize
should there have been any omissions or errors.